Nowell!
A Christmas Miscellany

Nowell!
A Christmas Miscellany

Sublime Words, Terrible Jokes, and Strange Facts
for the Festive Season

TIM DOWLEY

RESOURCE *Publications* · Eugene, Oregon

NOWELL! A CHRISTMAS MISCELLANY
Sublime Words, Terrible Jokes, and Strange Facts for the Festive Season

Resource Publications
An Imprint of Wipf and Stock Publishers
199 W. 8th Ave., Suite 3
Eugene, OR 97401

www.wipfandstock.com

PAPERBACK ISBN: 979-8-3852-1235-4
HARDCOVER ISBN: 979-8-3852-1236-1
EBOOK ISBN: 979-8-3852-1237-8

08/01/24

Permissions
New Revised Standard Version Bible, copyright 1989, Division of Christian Education of the National Council of the Churches of Christ in the United States of America. Used by permission. All rights reserved.
 "[little tree]" from *Tulips & Chimneys*, Copyright © 1923 by E. E. Cummings. Public Domain.
'God rest ye Unitarians', Chris Raible.

Illustrations
"The Adoration of the Magi" by Virgil Solis. © The Trustees of the British Museum, released as CC BY-NC-SA 4.0. Public Domain.
"The Nativity" by Hans Schäufelein. Creative Commons CC0 1.0 Universal Public Domain Dedication.
"Marley's Ghost" by John Leech. Public Domain.
"Christmas crackers" by Christian Wilhelm Allers. Public Domain.
"Old Christmas" by Robert Seymour. Public Domain.
"Putting Up the Christmas" by Frederick Walker. Public Domain.

Contents

THE POETRY OF CHRISTMAS

CHRISTMAS PRAYERS

Illustrations

Introduction

Joy to the world! the Lord is come:
Let earth receive her King!
Let ev'ry heart prepare him room,
And heav'n and nature sing![1]

Isaac Watts (1674–1748)

In *Christmas Miscellany*, I have gathered a rich mix of seasonally-themed pieces, with the intention that the reader will open the book serendipitously to discover a hitherto unknown quotation, a fascinating fact, or a joke that makes her wince. A "miscellany" amounts to a collection compiled from assorted writers and writings, organized around a common theme. Here to mine are numerous gems—it's worth digging to discover them. The reader never knows what she might next encounter.

I have been catholic in my choice, ranging from Scripture and the early church to twenty-first century authors. There are pieces from diverse churches and denominations and none, and contributions from many nations—though most originate in the U.S.A. and U.K. Inevitably there are copious quotations from the Victorians, who virtually invented Christmas as we know it—think Charles Dickens, Christina Rosetti, and Clement Moore . . . I've ranged far and wide in my search for entries, which extend from sacred poetry to terrible jokes; from seasonal prose and Scripture passages to diary quotations and extracts from letters and sermons; from

1. Keyte, *Carols*, p. 122.

holiday traditions to favorite Christmas movies, music, and songs. Among the many authors some unexpected names stand out—for instance Maya Angelou, Lewis Carroll, Anton Chekhov, Winston Churchill, George Eliot, Henry James, D. H. Lawrence, Samuel Pepys, J. K. Rowling, Dorothy L. Sayers, William Shakespeare, Leo Tolstoy, and George Washington.

Christmas Miscellany is intended both for personal enjoyment and reflection, and for use in seasonal carol services, and school and Sunday school festivities. This is a book to thumb through when searching for a colorful quote about Christmas feasting, a poem suitable for the Christmas carol service, or the words of a much-loved carol. You will find all of those here.

The entries are arranged by form, but if you're searching for specific writers or names you will find a full contents list, a list of authors, an index of titles, and a list of readings suitable for use at carol services and other seasonal celebrations.

Hopefully this little book, like the best Christmas carols, will transport the reader to a midwinter mood—filled with the aroma of mince pies, mulled wine, and lights twinkling on a tree.

O little town of Bethlehem,
How still we see thee lie!
Above thy deep and dreamless sleep
The silent stars go by.
Yet in thy dark streets shineth
The everlasting Light;
The hopes and fears of all the years
Are met in thee tonight.[2]

Phillips Brooks (1835–1893)

2. Keyte, *Carols*, p. 166.

Hymns for Advent

In many Christian churches Advent is a time of expectant waiting and preparation for the celebration of the birth of Christ—but also for the return of Christ at his Second Coming.

Of the Father's Love Begotten

Of the Father's love begotten
Ere the worlds began to be,
He is Alpha and Omega,
He the source, the ending he,
Of the things that are, that have been,
And that future years shall see,
Evermore and evermore.

O that birth forever blessèd,
When the Virgin, full of grace,
By the Holy Ghost conceiving,
Bore the Savior of our race,
And the Babe, the world's Redeemer,
First revealed his sacred face,
Evermore and evermore.

This is he whom seers and sages
Sang of old with one accord,
Whom the writings of the prophets
Promised in their faithful word;
Now he shines, the long-expected:
Let creation praise its Lord
Evermore and evermore.

O ye heights of heaven, adore him;
Angel hosts, his praises sing;
Powers, dominions, bow before him
And extol our God and King;
Let no tongue on earth be silent,
Every voice in concert ring,
Evermore and evermore.[1]

Probably the oldest known Christmas song still performed today, the Latin hymn *Corde natus*, by Aurelius Prudentius (348–413), a Christian lawyer living in Spain. Translated by John Mason Neale (1818–1866), Sir Henry W. Baker (1821–1877) and others.
Select stanzas.

1. *Ancient & Modern*, pp. 69, 727.

Come, Thou Long-expected Jesus

Come, thou long-expected Jesus,
Born to set thy people free;
From our fears and sins release us,
Let us find our rest in thee.

Israel's strength and consolation,
Hope of all the earth thou art;
Dear desire of every nation,
Joy of every longing heart.

Born thy people to deliver,
Born a child and yet a king;
Born to reign in us forever;
Now thy gracious kingdom bring.

By thy own eternal Spirit,
Rule in all our hearts alone:
By thy all-sufficient merit,
Raise us to thy glorious throne.[2]

Charles Wesley (1707–1788), English Methodist leader, author of
more than 6,500 hymns.

2. *Ancient & Modern*, p. 65.

Veni, veni, Emanuel

O come, O come, Emmanuel!
Redeem thy captive Israel
That into exile drear is gone,
Far from the face of God's dear Son.

Rejoice! rejoice! Emmanuel
Shall come to thee, O Israel.

O come, O come, thou Dayspring bright!
Pour on our souls thy healing light;
Dispel the long night's lingering gloom,
And pierce the shadows of the tomb.

O come, thou Key of David,[3] come,
And open wide our heavenly home;
Safeguard for us the heavenward road,
And bar the way to death's abode.

O come, O come, Adonaï,[4]
Who in thy glorious majesty
From Sinai's mountain, clothed in awe,
Gavest thy folk the elder Law.[5]

Select stanzas from a paraphrase of antiphons used at Vespers during the days before Christmas. Translated by John Mason Neale (1818–1866), English Episcopalian priest; revised by Thomas Alexander Lacey (1853–1931).

3. Isaiah 22:22.
4. "Lord", one of the titles Jewish people used to avoid the word "God."
5. Keyte, *Carols*, p. 17.

Joy to the World!

Joy to the world! the Lord is come:
Let earth receive her King!
Let ev'ry heart prepare him room,
And heav'n and nature sing.

Joy to the earth! the Savior reigns:
Let men their songs employ,
While fields and floods, rocks, hills, and plains
Repeat the sounding joy.

He rules the world with truth and grace,
And makes the nations prove
The glories of his righteousness,
And wonders of his love.[6]

Paraphrase of Psalm 98 by Isaac Watts, (1674–1748), English
hymnwriter and inveterate rhymester.
Select verses.

---

6. Keyte, *Carols*, p. 123.

Hark! the Herald Angels Sing

Hark! the herald angels sing:
"Glory to the new-born King!
Peace on earth and mercy mild,
God and sinners reconciled!"
Joyful, all ye nations, rise!
Join the triumph of the skies!
With th'angelic host proclaim:
"Christ is born in Bethlehem!"

Hail! the heav'n-born Prince of Peace!
Hail the Sun of Righteousness!
Light and life to all he brings,
Ris'n with healing in his wings.
Mild, he lays his glory by,
Born that man no more may die,
Born to raise the sons of earth,
Born to give them second birth.[7]

Charles Wesley (1707–1788), adapted by George Whitefield
(1714–1770), English evangelist.
Select verses.

7. Keyte, *Carols*, p. 146.

A CHRISTMAS CALENDAR

11 November: Martinmas Day: A day of feasting when livestock were killed for winter consumption.

Stir-up Sunday: the last Sunday before the First Advent Sunday. The name derives from the opening words of the collect for the day in the Episcopalian Book of Common Prayer: "Stir up, we beseech thee, O Lord, the wills of thy faithful people". By tradition, the Christmas pudding is mixed on this day.

Advent Sunday: the beginning of the season of Advent.

Last Saturday in November: In the Netherlands, *Sinterklaas* (St. Nicholas) arrives by boat.

About this time: The first of four Advent Sundays.

5 December: In the Netherlands, *Sinterklaas* Eve, when children often receive their gifts.

6 December: St. Nicholas' Day. In parts of Europe, the saint visits homes and brings presents for good children. In some countries he also delivers the Christmas tree. In medieval England choirboys elected one of their company as boy bishop.

8 December: Feast of the Immaculate Conception. In Spain, this marks the beginning of Christmas.

13 December: St. Lucy of Syracuse, or St. Lucia. In Sweden, Norway, and parts of Finland, a festival of lights.

16 December: Start of *Posadas* in Mexico and South American countries, when processions re-enact Mary and Joseph's search for shelter.

21 December: St. Thomas' Day. In medieval England parishioners gave money to poor elderly neighbors—a practice known as "Thomasing" or "mumping".

21/22 December: Winter solstice. The shortest, darkest day of the year—linked with pagan customs relating to death, rebirth, and the survival of the sun.

24 December: Christmas Eve. Midnight Mass celebrated. In earlier centuries, this marked the end of the Christmas fast. In many parts of Europe, the main Christmas meal is eaten and gifts are received.

25 December: Christmas Day. In the English-speaking world, Christmas dinner is eaten and gifts are exchanged. First of the Twelve Days of Christmas.

26 December: St. Stephen's Day—the first Christian martyr. Also known as Boxing Day.

27 December: St. John the Evangelist.

28 December: Holy Innocents' Day, or Childermas. Remembering the infant boys slaughtered by Herod. In Spain, people play tricks on one another. In some places the boy bishop, elected on St. Nicholas' Day, reigned for the day.

31 December: New Year's Eve, in Germany St Sy(i)lvester's Day. Hogmanay in Scotland. Celebrated by eating, drinking, and fireworks. In some places, all the windows were flung open at midnight to let out the old year.

1 January: New Year's Day and Feast of the Circumcision of Jesus, or Holy Name of Jesus.

5 January: Epiphany Eve.

6 January: Epiphany—the arrival of the Magi at the Bethlehem stable. In Ireland known as Women's Christmas. Twelfth Night: the Twelve Days of Christmas end and the Christmas tree should have been taken down. In Italy, children receive a stocking filled with sweets—or coal if they've misbehaved

First Monday after Epiphany: Plow Monday. The beginning of new working year for men, who started plowing again.

First Tuesday after Epiphany: St. Distaff's Day. The beginning of new working year for women, who resumed spinning.

2 February: Candlemas—Commemorates presentation of Jesus at the Temple in Jerusalem. In America, "Groundhog Day". Until Victorian times, decorations were taken down. Candles and fires were lit. Final goodbye to Christmas.

SOME CHRISTMAS TRADITIONS

The yule log was orginally a carefully selected tree, brought into the house with ceremony to be burnt over the twelve days of Christmas.

The Christmas cracker was invented by London candy-store owner Tom Smith (1823–1869) in 1847, after seeing in Paris sugared almond *bon-bons* wrapped in tissue twisted at each end. He started to sell wrapped sweets with a motto inside, later adding a trinket and banger strip—hence the onomatopoeic "cracker".

The first commercial Christmas card was commissioned in London in 1843 by civil servant Sir Henry Cole (1808–1882). A hand-colored lithograph illustration by John Callcott Horsley (1817–1903) depicted an English family Christmas party.

Since 1947 Norway has sent a Christmas tree to stand in London's Trafalgar Square, in thanks for British assistance during World War II.

Christmas Elsewhere

Captain Cook's Christmas

24 December 1769

Land in sight, an Island or rather several small ones most probably 3 Kings, so that it was conjecturd that we had Passd the Cape which had so long troubled us. Calm most of the Day: myself in a boat shooting in which I had good success, killing cheifly several Gannets or Solan Geese so like European ones that they are hardly distinguishable from them. As it was the humour of the ship to keep Christmas in the old fashiond way, it was resolvd of them to make a Goose pye for tomorrows dinner.

25 December

Christmas day: Our Goose pye was eat with great approbation and in the Evening all hands were as Drunk as our forefathers usd to be upon the like occasion.

26 December

This morn all heads achd with yesterdays debauch. Wind has been Easterly these 3 or 4 days so we have not got at all nearer the Island than we were.[8]

The *Endeavour*, under Captain James Cook, sailed west from Tahiti in search of the unknown continent of Australia.

8. Beaglehole, *Endeavour* pp. 448–449.

Christmas Eve in Dresden

In the evening we witnessed some of the results of this very peculiar national feeling and custom; that, I mean, of the children giving presents to the parents and the parents to the children on Christmas Eve . . . . [A] little bell rang, and we went into the room where the presents which the children had secretly prepared for the elder members of the family were placed under the tree. They were all prepared by two little girls of twelve and fourteen . . . and though there was nothing very valuable or beautiful in what was given, yet it was all received with so much pleasure by the parents and elder brother, that the children were delighted, and kissed us all round very heartily. While this was going on a bell rang in another part of the house, and we were led through a passage-way purposely kept dark, where two folding-doors were thrown open and we were all at once in a large and handsome saloon, which was brilliantly lighted up, and where were the presents which the parents had provided for the children.[9]

An American, George Tickner, describes Christmas at Baron Ungern Sternberg's house in Dresden, Germany, 1835.

9. Hadfield, *Twelve Days*, p. 102.

Midnight Mass in France

We started off, a number of us, together in a stream of light, which I called the glow-worm procession, over a road that at this nocturnal hour was not lacking in solemnity—the long avenue leading out from the park to the church. Our lanterns cast great shadows on the white road, crisp with frost which crackled under my feet as I walked . . . .

As our little group advanced, it saw others on the way, people from the farm and from the mill, who joined us, and, once on the Place de l'Église, we found ourselves with all the parishioners in a body. No one spoke—the icy north wind cut short our breath; but the voice of the chimes filled the silence. . . .

Above us the stars shone like diamond nails driven into velvet, and my eyes sought confidently the most beautiful, the one that guided the Wise Men, convinced as I was that it must guide us too, and all who are good. The old church, out of all proportion to the village of four hundred souls it sheltered, rose much more majestically than in the broad daylight; and how black was its ivy-mantled tower, which is all that remains to it from the thirteenth century! We entered, accompanied by a gust of wind that swept into the porch at the same time as we did; and the splendours of the altar, studded with lights, green with pine and laurel branches, dazzled us from the threshold . . . .[10]

Mme. Th. Bentzen recalls her childhood in rural France, around 1850.

10. Hadfield, *Twelve Days*, p. 71.

A Gigantic Mistake

A very merry Christmas, with roast beef in a violent perspiration, and the thermometer 110 deg. in the shade!

A remarkably merry Christmas, with the hot wind raging, and one's plate of Christmas cheer two fork-handles-deep in gravel! An excessively merry Christmas for John Shepherd, as he sits in the shade of his cabbage-tree hat on the burnt-up grass of the Tartarus Plains, and munches his bread and mutton wearily, while the sheep lie in panting groups, strung out under the haze....

It may be rank heresy, but I deliberately affirm that Christmas in Australia is a gigantic mistake.[11]

Marcus Clarke (1846–1881), from the *Australasian,* 26 December 1868.

---

11. Santich, *Magic Pudding,* p. 26

Christmas in Moscow

23 December 1858

Came to Moscow with the children. Didn't manage to get another mortgage. Money is needed everywhere. Went bear-hunting. On the 21st—killed one; on the 22nd—was bitten by one. Squandered a pile of money.[12]

Leo Tolstoy (1828–1910), Russian novelist, author of *War and Peace*.

12. *American Scholar*, p. 1.

Christmas Day in the Antarctic

. . . I had observed Shackleton ferreting about in his bundle, out of which he presently produced a spare sock, and stowed away in the toe of that sock was a small round object about the size of a cricket ball, which, when brought to light, proved to be a noble "plum-pudding". Another dive into his lucky-bag and out came a crumpled piece of artificial holly. Heated in the cocoa, our plum-pudding was soon steaming hot, and stood on the cooker-lid crowned with its decoration.[13]

Captain Robert Falcon Scott (1868–1912), during his unsuccessful attempt to reach the South Pole, 1902.

13. Scott, *Discovery*, p. 48

The Christmas Truce

Nobody can tell you the whole true story of that incredible Christmas truce of the First World War . . . The Germans unquestionably began it—almost certainly the Saxons. . . . Men of the North Staffordshire Regiment found themselves exchanging "words of good cheer" with their opposite numbers. Then they got up and sat on the parapet, talking across No Man's Land to each other. A British officer suggested a *Volkslied*. The Germans agreed eagerly, both sides singing in turn . . . . A truce was agreed upon until midnight on Christmas Day. It took the shape at first of both sides helping one another to bury their dead.

In another part of the line the troops walked about arm in arm, photographing each other, while the Germans facing a Highland Regiment began by a cornet player rendering "Home Sweet Home" perfectly, followed by a hymn tune. They then got out of their trenches and walking smilingly towards the Scots. When an officer tried to stop them they said rather pathetically—"But this is Christmas—aren't you Scotsmen Christians too?"

It ended half diffidently—a gradual return to the normality of killing each other—with both sides firing warning shots in the air.[14]

The Western Front, 1914.
Anonymous.

---

14. Hadfield, *Twelve Days*, p. 114.

Christmas 1917

Although the battalion was in the line, we determined to see that Christmas was properly observed. I was elected Master of Ceremonies of B Company. (Few Padres escaped this.) I made friends with the cook, and together we drew up the menu and produced the following remarkable effusion:

Xmas Day Menu
Soups *Maitre de* Dugout
Poisson Pilchard *dans la Boite*
Bulle au Boeuf
Pouding Noel
The King   Absent Friends[15]

Revd. B. Hinchliffe, Chaplain, Northumberland Fusiliers.

15. Macdonald, *Voices*, p. 257.

CHRISTMAS CRACKER HUMOR

Christmas dinner

How do you drain your Christmas brussels sprouts?
With an Advent colander.

Who's never hungry at Christmas?
The turkey—he's always stuffed.

What do you get if you eat Christmas decorations?
Tinsillitis.

Why aren't elves allowed Christmas dinner?
Because they're always goblin their food.

Mommy, can I have a puppy for Christmas?
No—you can have turkey like everyone else.

Sheep—but no goats

What do sheep put in their Christmas cards?
Merry Christmas to Ewe.

What did the sheep say to the shepherd?
Season's bleatings.

What do cats put on their Christmas cards?
Wishing you a furry Merry Christmas and a Happy Mew Year.

What do wild animals sing at Christmas?
Jungle Bells, Jungle Bells . . .

Who delivers cats' Christmas presents?
Santa Paws.

Carol Groans

There was a young woman called White
Who sang carols with all her might;
She would ring someone's bell
And warble Nowell
Till they begged her for "Silent Night".

How does King Wenceslas like his pizza?
Deep-pan, crisp, and even.

Which carol is popular in the desert?
O Camel Ye Faithful.

What does Dracula sing at Christmas?
I'm dreaming of a Fright Christmas.

What's the hairdressers' favorite carol?
O Comb All Ye Faithful.

The Poetry of Christmas

I sing of a maiden

I sing of a maiden
That is makeles:[16]
King of alle kinges
To here son she ches.[17]

He cam also[18] stille
Ther his moder[19] was,
As dew in Aprille
That falleth on the grass.

He cam also stille
To his moder's bowr,
As dew in Aprille
That falleth on the flowr.

He cam also stille
Ther his moder lay,
As dew in Aprille
That falleth on the spray.

Moder and maiden
Was never non but she:
Well may swich[20] a lady
Godes moder be.[21]

Fifteenth-century English celebration of the Annunciation.
Anonymous.

16. matchless.
17. She chose for her son.
18. as.
19. mother.
20. such.
21. Davies, *English Lyrics*, p. 155

The Burning Babe

As I in hoary winter's night stood shivering in the snow,
Surprised I was with sudden heat which made my heart to glow;
And lifting up a fearful eye to view what fire was near,
A pretty Babe all burning bright did in the air appear;
Who, scorchèd with excessive heat, such floods of tears did shed,
As though his floods should quench his flames which with his
tears were fed.
"Alas!" quoth he, "but newly born in fiery heats I fry,
Yet none approach to warm their hearts or feel my fire but I.
My faultless breast the furnace is, the fuel wounding thorns;
Love is the fire, and sighs the smoke, the ashes shame and scorns;
The fuel justice layeth on, and mercy blows the coals;
The metal in this furnace wrought are men's defilèd souls:
For which, as now on fire I am to work them to their good,
So will I melt into a bath to wash them in my blood."
With this he vanished out of sight and swiftly shrunk away,
And straight I callèd unto mind that it was Christmas day.[22]

Robert Southwell (1561–1595), Jesuit poet and clandestine
missionary to Elizabethan England.

22. Batchelor, *Christian Poetry*, p. 273.

New Prince, New Pomp

Behold, a silly[23] tender Babe
In freezing winter night
In homely manger trembling lies,
Alas, a piteous sight!

The inns are full; no man will yield
This little pilgrim bed,
But forced he is with silly beasts
In crib to shroud his head.

Despise him not for lying there,
First, what he is inquire:
An orient pearl is often found
In depth of dirty mire.

Weigh not his crib, his wooden dish,
Nor beasts that by him feed;
Weigh not his Mother's poor attire
Nor Joseph's simple weed.[24]

This stable is a Prince's court,
This crib his chair of state;
The beasts are parcel of his pomp,
The wooden dish his plate.

The persons in that poor attire
His royal liveries wear;
The Prince himself is come from heaven;
This pomp is prizèd there.

23. weak, helpless.
24. clothes.

With joy approach, O Christian wight,[25]
Do homage to thy King;
And highly praise his humble pomp,
Which he from heaven doth bring.[26]

Robert Southwell

25. being, creature.
26. Gardner, *English Verse*, p. 101.

Our Lady's Lullaby

Upon my lap my Sovereign sits,
And sucks upon my breast;
Meanwhile, his love sustains my life,
And gives my body rest.
Sing lullaby, my little Boy,
Sing lullaby, my lifes Joy!

When thou hast taken thy repast
Repose, my Babe, on me;
So may thy mother and thy nurse
Thy cradle also be.

My Babe, my Bliss, my Child, my Choice,
My Fruit, My flower, and Bud,
My Jesus, and my only Joy,
The Sum of all my good.[27]

Richard Rowlands, born Verstegen, (c. 1550–1640), Anglo-Dutch
writer.
Select stanzas.

---

27. Lewis, *Christmas*, p. 137.

A Hymn on the Nativity of my Saviour

I sing the birth was born tonight,
The author both of life and light;
The angels so did sound it,
And like the ravished shepherds said,
Who saw the light, and were afraid,
Yet searched, and true they found it.

The Son of God, th'eternal King,
That did us all salvation bring,
And freed the soul from danger;
He whom the whole world could not take,
The Word which heaven and earth did make,
Was now laid in a manger.

The Father's wisdom willed it so,
The Son's obedience knew no "No",
Both wills were one in stature;
And as that wisdom had decreed,
The Word was now made flesh indeed,
And took on him our nature.

What comfort by him do we win
Who made himself the price of sin,
To make us heirs of glory?
To see this babe, all innocence,
A martyr born in our defence,
Can man forget this story?[28]

Ben Jonson (1572–1637), English playwright.
Jonson asserted if "he had written . . . 'The Burning Babe' [by Southwell], he would have been content to destroy many of his".

28. Cain, *Jonson*, p. 772.

Nativitie

Immensity cloysterd in thy deare wombe,
Now leaves his welbelov'd imprisonment,
There he hath made himselfe to his intent
Weake enough, now into our world to come;
But Oh, for thee, for him, hath th'Inne no roome?
Yet lay him in this stall, and from the Orient,
Starres, and wisemen will travell to prevent
Th'effect of Herods jealous generall doome.
See'st thou, my Soule, with thy faiths eyes, how he
Which fils all place, yet none holds him, doth lye?
Was not his pity towards thee wondrous high,
That would have need to be pittied by thee?
Kiss him, and with him into Egypt goe,
With his kinde mother, who partakes thy woe.[29]

From *La Corona*, John Donne (1572–1631), English poet and priest.

---

29. Hayward, *John Donne*, p. 164.

NOWELL! A CHRISTMAS MISCELLANY

The Angels for the Nativity of our Lord

Run, shepherds, run, where Bethlem blest appears,
We bring the best of news, be not dismayed,
A Saviour there is born more old than years,
Amidst heaven's rolling heights this earth who stayed.
In a poor cottage inned, a virgin maid
A weakling did him bear, who all upbears;
There is he, poorly swaddled, in manger laid,
To whom too narrow swaddlings are our spheres:
Run, shepherds, run, and solemnize his birth.
This is that night—no, day, grown great with bliss,
In which the power of Satan broken is;
In heaven be glory, peace unto the Earth!
    Thus singing, through the air the angels swarm,
    And cope of stars re-echoèd the same.[30]

William Drummond of Hawthornden (1585–1649), Scottish poet.

30. Batchelor, *Christian Poetry*, p. 283.

A Christmas Carolle, sung to the King in the Presence at White-Hall

What sweeter musick can we bring,
Than a caroll for to sing
The Birth of this our heavenly King?...

Dark and dull night, flie hence away,
And give the honour of this Day,
That sees December turned to May . . .

The Darling of the world is come,
And fit it is, we finde a roome
To welcome Him. The nobler part
Of all the house here, is the heart,

Which we will give Him; and bequeath
This Hollie and this Ivie Wreath,
To do Him honour, who's our King
And Lord of all this Revelling.[31]

Robert Herrick (1591–1674), English poet.

31. Martin, *Herrick*, p. 364.

On the Infancy of our Saviour

Hail, blessed Virgin, full of heavenly grace,
Blest above all that sprang from human race;
Whose heaven-saluted womb brought forth in one,
A blessed Saviour, and a blessed son:
Oh! what a ravishment it had been to see
Thy little Saviour perking on thy knee!
To see him nuzzle in thy virgin breast,
His milk-white body all unclad, undressed!
To see thy busy fingers clothe and wrap
His spradling limbs in thy indulgent lap!
To see his desperate eyes, with childish grace,
Smiling upon his smiling mother's face!
And, when his forward strength began to bloom,
To see him diddle up and down the room!
Oh, who would think so sweet a babe as this
Should e'er be slain by a false-hearted kiss!
Had I a rag, if sure thy body wore it,
Pardon, sweet Babe, I think I should adore it:
Till then, O grant this boon (a boon far dearer),
The weed not being, I may adore the wearer.[32]

Francis Quarles (1592–1644), English poet.

---

32. Batchelor, *Christian Poetry*, p., 278.

Christmas

All after pleasures as I rid one day,
My horse and I, both tir'd, in bodie and minde,
With full crie of affections, quite astray;
I took up in the next inne I could finde.

There when I came, whom found I but my deare,
My dearest Lord, expecting till the grief
Of pleasures brought me to him, readie there
To be all passengers most sweet relief?

O Thou, whose glorious, yet contracted light,
Wrapt in night's mantle, stole into a manger;
Since my dark soul and brutish is thy right,
To Man of all beasts be not thou a stranger:

Furnish and deck my soul, that thou mayst have
A better lodging, then a rack, or grave.[33]

George Herbert (1593–1633), English cleric and poet.
First part.

---

33. Levi, *Christian Verse*, p. 108.

Ode on the Morning of Christ's Nativity

This is the month, and this the happy morn,
Wherein the Son of heaven's eternal King,
Of wedded maid and virgin mother born,
Our great redemption from above did bring;
For so the holy sages once did sing,
That he our deadly forfeit should release,
And with his Father work us a perpetual peace.

That glorious form, that light unsufferable,
And that far-beaming blaze of majesty,
Wherewith he wont at heaven's high council-table
To sit the midst of trinal unity,
He laid aside; and here with us to be,
Forsook the courts of everlasting day,
And chose with us a darksome house of mortal clay.

Say, heavenly muse, shall not thy sacred vein
Afford a present to the infant God?
Hast thou no verse, no hymn, or solemn strain,
To welcome him to this his new abode,
Now while the heaven, by the sun's team untrod,
Hath took no print of the approaching light,
And all the spangled host keep watch in squadrons bright?

See how from far upon the eastern road
The star-led wizards haste with odours sweet!
O run, prevent them with thy humble ode,
And lay it lowly at his blessed feet;
Have thou the honour first thy Lord to greet,
And join thy voice unto the angel quire,
From out his secret altar touched with hallowed fire.[34]

34. Batchelor, *Christian Poetry*, p. 265.

John Milton (1608–1674), English poet, author of *Paradise Lost*. Select stanzas.

Upon Christ His Birth

Strange news! a Cittie full? Will none give way
To lodge a guest that comes not every day?
Noe inne, nor taverne void? yet I descry
One empty place alone, where wee may ly:
In too much fullnesse is some want: but where?
Men's empty hearts: let's ask for lodgeing there.
But if they not admit us, then wee'le say
Their hearts, as well as inns, are made of clay.[35]

Sir John Suckling (1609–1641), English Cavalier poet—and
inventor of the card game cribbage.

35. Clayton, *Suckling*, p. 9.

Hymn

Lord, when the wise men came from far
Led to thy cradle by a star,
Then did the shepherds too rejoice,
Instructed by thy angel's voice:
Blest were the wise men in their skill,
And shepherds in their harmless will.

Wise men, in tracing nature's laws,
Ascend unto the highest cause;
Shepherds with humble fearfulness
Walk safely, though their light be less.
Though wise men better know the way,
It seems no honest heart can stray.

There is no merit in the wise
But love, the shepherds' sacrifice.
Wise men, all ways of knowledge passed,
To the shepherds' wonder come at last:
To know can only wonder breed,
And not to know is wonder's seed.[36]

Sidney Godolphin (1610–1643), English poet, killed in the English
Civil War.
Select stanzas.

36. Batchelor, *Christian Poetry*, p. 289.

"The Adoration of the Magi", woodcut by Virgil Solis, after 1552.

That the Great Angel-blinding Light

That the great angell-blinding Light should shrinke
His blaze, to shine in a poore shepherd's eye:
That the unmeasur'd God so low should sinke,
As prison'r in a few poore rags to lye:
That from His mother's brest He milke should drinke,
Who feeds with nectar Heav'n's faire family:
That a vile manger His low bed should prove,
Who in a throne of stars thunders above.

That He Whom the sun serves, should faintly peepe
Through clouds of infant flesh; that He the old
Eternall Word should be a child, and weepe:
That He Who made the fire, should feare the cold:
That Heav'n's high Majesty His court should keepe
In a clay-cottage, by each blast control'd:
That Gloryie's Self should serve our griefs and feares,
And free Eternity, submit to yeares.[37]

XXII, XXIII, from "Satan", by Richard Crashaw (c. 1613–1649), English poet who converted from Anglicanism to Roman Catholicism.

37. Grosart, *Crashaw*, p. 103.

A Hymne of the Nativity, sung by the Shepherds

Gloomy Night embract the place
Where the noble infant lay:
The babe lookt up and shew'd his face,
In spight of darknesse it was day.
It was thy Day, Sweet, and did rise,
Not from the East, but from thine eyes.

Winter chid the world, and sent
The angry North to wage his warres.
The North forgot his fierce intent,
And left perfumes, instead of scarres.
By those sweet Eyes persuasive Powers
Where he meant frosts, he scattered Flowers . . .

Wellcome, all Wonders in one sight!
Æternity shutt in a span.
Sommer in Winter, Day in Night,
Heaven in earth, and GOD in MAN.
Great little one! whose all-embracing birth
Lifts earth to heaven, stoopes heav'n to earth.[38]

Richard Crashaw.
Select stanzas.

38. Williams, *Crashaw*, pp. 78, 83.

"The Nativity", print by Hans Schäufelein, 1514.

A Cradle Song

Hush! my dear, lie still and slumber,
Holy Angels guard thy bed!
Heavenly blessings without number
Gently falling on thy head.

Sleep, my babe; thy food and raiment,
House and home, thy friends provide;
All without thy care or payment,
All thy wants are well supplied.

How much better thou'rt attended
Than the Son of God could be,
When from heaven he descended,
And became a child like thee!

Soft and easy is thy cradle:
Coarse and hard thy Saviour lay:
When his birthplace was a stable,
And his softest bed was hay.

Lo, he slumbers in his manger,
Where the hornèd oxen fed;
—Peace, my darling, here's no danger;
Here's no ox a-near thy bed.[39]

Isaac Watts (1674–1748), English cleric and hymnwriter.
Select stanzas.

---

39. Batchelor, *Christian Poetry*, p. 433.

A Christmas Carol

The shepherds went their hasty way,
And found the lowly stable-shed
Where the Virgin-Mother lay:
And now they checked their eager tread,
For to the Babe, that at her bosom clung,
A Mother's song the Virgin-Mother sung.

They told her how a glorious light,
Streaming from a heavenly throng,
Around them shone, suspending night!
While sweeter than a mother's song,
Blest Angels heralded the Saviour's birth,
Glory to God on high! and Peace on Earth.

She listened to the tale divine,
And closer still the Babe she pressed;
And while she cried, the Babe is mine!
The milk rushed faster to her breast:
Joy rose within her, like a summer's morn;
Peace, Peace on Earth! the Prince of Peace is born.[40]

Samuel Taylor Coleridge (1772–1834), English poet, author of
"The Rime of the Ancient Mariner".
An excerpt.

40. Coleridge, *Poetical Works*, p. 338.

A Cradle Song

Sweet dreams form a shade
O'er my lovely infant's head:
Sweet dreams of pleasant streams
By happy, silent moony beams.

Sweet babe, in thy face
Holy image I can trace:
Sweet babe, once like thee
Thy Maker lay and wept for me.

Wept for me, for thee, for all
When He was an infant small:
Thou His image ever see,
Heavenly face that smiles on thee.

Smiles on me, on thee, on all,
Who became an infant small:
Infant smiles are His own smiles,
Heaven and earth to peace beguiles.[41]

William Blake (1757–1827), English poet and painter.
Select stanzas.

41. Brooks-Davies, *Christmas Please!*, p. 6.

Christmas Bells

I heard the bells on Christmas Day
Their old familiar carols play,
And wild and sweet
The words repeat
Of "Peace on earth, good will to men!"

And thought how, as the day had come,
The belfries of all Christendom
Had rolled along
The unbroken song,
Of "Peace on earth, good will to men!"

Till, ringing, singing on its way,
The world revolved from night to day—
A voice, a chime,
A chant sublime
Of "Peace on earth, good will to men!"[42]

Henry Wadsworth Longfellow (1807–1882).
Select stanzas.

---

42. Batchelor, *Christian Poetry*, p. 268.

The Time Draws Near the Birth of Christ

The time draws near the birth of Christ:
The moon is hid; the night is still;
The Christmas bells from hill to hill
Answer each other in the mist.

Four voices of four hamlets round,
From far and near, on mead and moor,
Swell out and fail, as if a door
Were shut between me and the sound:

Each voice four changes on the wind,
That now dilate, and now decrease,
Peace and goodwill, goodwill and peace,
Peace and goodwill, to all mankind.

This year I slept and woke with pain,
I almost wished no more to wake,
And that my hold on life would break
Before I heard those bells again:

But they my troubled spirit rule,
For they controll'd me when a boy;
They bring me sorrow touched with joy.
The merry merry bells of Yule.[43]

Alfred Lord Tennyson (1809–1892), Section XXVIII from his lengthy narrative poem, "In Memoriam A. H. H.", an elegy for a university friend.

---

43. Tennnyson, *Poems*, p. 888.

Music on Christmas Morning

Music I love—but never strain
Could kindle raptures so divine,
So grief assuage, so conquer pain,
And rouse this pensive heart of mine—
As that we hear on Christmas morn,
Upon the wintry breezes borne.

Though Darkness still her empire keep,
And hours must pass, ere morning break;
From troubled dreams, or slumbers deep,
That music *kindly* bids us wake;
It calls us, with an angel's voice,
To wake, and worship, and rejoice;

To greet with joy the glorious morn,
Which angels welcomed long ago,
When our redeeming Lord was born,
To bring the light of Heaven below;
The Powers of Darkness to dispel,
And rescue Earth from Death and Hell.

While listening to that sacred strain,
My raptured spirit soars on high;
I seem to hear those songs again
Resounding through the open sky,
That kindled such divine delight,
In those who watched their flocks by night.[44]

Anne Brontë (1820–1849), English novelist, author of *The Tenant of Wildfell Hall.*
Select stanzas.

44. Chitham, *Brontë*, p. 96.

Christmastide

Love came down at Christmas,
Love all lovely, Love Divine;
Love was born at Christmas,
Star and Angels gave the sign.

Worship we the Godhead,
Love Incarnate, Love Divine;
Worship we our Jesus:
But wherewith for sacred sign?

Love shall be our token,
Love be yours and love be mine,
Love to God and all men,
Love for plea and gift and sign.[45]

Christina Rossetti (1830–1894), English author.

45. Crump, Rossetti, p. 215.

Christmas Day and Every Day

Star high,
Baby low:
'Twixt the two
Wise men go;
Find the baby,
Grasp the star—
Heirs of all things
Near and far![46]

George Macdonald (1824–1905), Scottish author, described by
C. S. Lewis as his "master".

46. Hyett, *Christmas Poems*, p. 11.

Christmas Everywhere

Everywhere, everywhere, Christmas to-night!
Christmas in lands of the fir tree and pine,
Christmas in lands of the palm tree and vine;
Christmas where snow-peaks stand solemn and white,
Christmas where corn-fields stand sunny and bright;
Everywhere, everywhere, Christmas to-night!

Christmas where children are hopeful and gay,
Christmas where old men are patient and gray;
Christmas where peace, like a dove in its flight,
Broods o'er brave men in the thick of the fight;
Everywhere, everywhere, Christmas to-night!

For the Christ-child who comes is the master of all,
No palace too great, no cottage too small;
The Angels who welcome Him sing from the height,
"In the city of David a King in His might."
Everywhere, everywhere, Christmas to-night![47]

Phillips Brooks (1835–1893), author of "O little town of Bethlehem".

47. Brooks, *Christmas Songs*, p. 17.

Yuletide in a Younger World

We believed in highdays then,
And could glimpse at night
On Christmas Eve
Imminent oncomings of radiant revel—
Doings of delight—
Now we have no such sight.

We had eyes for phantoms then,
And at bridge or stile
On Christmas Eve
Clear beheld those countless ones who had crossed it
Cross again in file:—
Such has ceased longwhile!

We liked divination then,
And, as they homeward wound
On Christmas Eve,
We could read men's dreams within them spinning
Even as wheels spin round—
Now we are blinker-bound.

We heard still small voices then,
And, in the dim serene
Of Christmas Eve,
Caught the fartime tones of fire-filled prophets
Long on earth unseen...
—Can such ever have been?[48]

Thomas Hardy (1840–1928), English novelist and poet.

48. Hynes: *Hardy*, p. 437.

Christmas Eve

Alone—with one fair star for company,
The loveliest star among the hosts of night,
While the grey tide ebbs with the ebbing light—
I pace along the darkening wintry sea.
Now round the yule-log and the glittering tree
Twinkling with festive tapers, eyes as bright
Sparkle with Christmas joys and young delight,
As each one gathers to his family.

But I—a waif on earth where'er I roam—
Uprooted with life's bleeding hopes and fears
From that one heart that was my heart's sole home,
Feel the old pang pierce through the severing years,
And as I think upon the years to come
That fair star trembles through my falling tears.[49]

Mathilde Blind (1841–1896), German-born English poet.

49. Blind, *Songs*, p. 116

Salus Mundi[50]

I saw a stable, low and very bare,
A little child in a manger.
The oxen knew him, had him in their care,
To men he was a stranger.
The safety of the world was lying there,
And the world's danger.[51]

Mary Elizabeth Coleridge (1861–1907), British poet and novelist.

50. The safety of the world.
51. Batchelor, *Christian Poetry*, p. 260.

Chrismus Is A-Comin'

Bones a-gittin' achy,
Back a-feelin' col',
Han's a-growin' shaky,
Jes' lak I was ol'.
Fros' erpon de meddah
Lookin' mighty white;
Snowdraps lak a feddah
Slippin' down at night.
Jes' keep t'ings a-hummin'
Spite o' fros' an' showahs,
Chrismus is a-comin'
An' all de week is ouahs.

Dey'll be banjo pickin',
Dancin' all night thoo.
Dey'll be lots o' chicken,
Plenty tukky, too.
Drams to wet yo' whistles
So's to drive out the chills.
Whut I keer fu' drizzles
Fallin' on de hills?
Jes' keep t'ings a-hummin'
Spite o' col' an' showahs,
Chrismus day's a-comin',
An' all de week is ouahs.[52]

Paul Laurence Dunbar (1872–1906), African American poet, son
of enslaved parents.
Select stanzas.

---

52. Dunbar, *Poems*.

How Far to Bethlehem?

How far is it to Bethlehem?
Not very far.
Shall we find the stable-room
Lit by a star?

Can we see the little Child,
Is He within?
If we lift the wooden latch,
May we go in?

May we stroke the creatures there,
Ox, ass and sheep?
May we peep like them and see
Jesus asleep?

If we touch His tiny hand
Will he awake?
Will He know we've come so far
Just for His sake?

Great Kings have precious gifts
And we have naught;
Little smiles and little tears
Are all we brought.

For all weary children
Mary must weep.
Here on his bed of straw
Sleep, children, sleep.

God in his mother's arms,
Babes in the byre
Sleep as they sleep who find
Their heart's desire.[53]

Frances Chesterton (1869–1938), English author, wife of G. K. Chesterton.

53. Chesterton, *Bethlehem*, p. 5.

The House of Christmas

There fared a mother driven forth
Out of an inn to roam;
In the place where she was homeless
All men are at home.
The crazy stable close at hand,
With shaking timber and shifting sand,
Grew a stronger thing to abide and stand
Than the square stones of Rome.

For men are homesick in their homes,
And strangers under the sun,
And they lay their heads in a foreign land
Whenever the day is done.
Here we have battle and blazing eyes,
And chance and honour and high surprise,
But our homes are under miraculous skies
Where the yule tale was begun.

A Child in a foul stable,
Where the beasts feed and foam;
Only where He was homeless
Are you and I at home;
We have hands that fashion and heads that know,
But our hearts we lost—how long ago!
In a place no chart nor ship can show
Under the sky's dome.

This world is wild as an old wives' tale,
And strange the plain things are,
The earth is enough and the air is enough
For our wonder and our war;
But our rest is as far as the fire-drake swings
And our peace is put in impossible things
Where clashed and thundered unthinkable wings
Round an incredible star.

To an open house in the evening
Home shall men come,
To an older place than Eden
And a taller town than Rome.
To the end of the way of the wandering star,
To the things that cannot be and that are,
To the place where God was homeless
And all men are at home.[54]

G. K. Chesterton (1874–1936), English author and Christian apologist, "prince of paradox".

---

54. Chesterton, *Christmas*, p. 35.

A Christmas Carol

The Christ-child lay on Mary's lap,
His hair was like a light.
(O weary, weary were the world,
But here is all aright.)

The Christ-child lay on Mary's breast,
His hair was like a star.
(O stern and cunning are the kings,
But here the true hearts are.)

The Christ-child lay on Mary's heart,
His hair was like a fire.
(O weary, weary is the world,
But here the world's desire.)

The Christ-child stood at Mary's knee,
His hair was like a crown.
And all the flowers looked up at Him,
And all the stars looked down.

G. K. Chesterton[55].

55. Chesterton, *Christmas*, p. 13.

The Friendly Beasts

Jesus, our brother, kind and good,
Was humbly born in a stable rude,
And the friendly beasts around Him stood;
Jesus, our brother, strong and good.

"I," said the donkey, shaggy and brown,
"I carried his mother up hill and down
I carried her safely to Bethlehem town;
I," said the donkey, shaggy and brown.

"I," said the cow, all white and red,
"I gave Him my manger for His bed,
I gave Him my hay to pillow His head;
I," said the cow, all white and red.

"I," said the sheep with curly horn,
"I gave Him my wool for His blanket warm,
He wore my coat on Christmas morn;
I," said the sheep with curly horn.

"I," said the dove from the rafters high,
"I cooed him to sleep that He should not cry,
We cooed him to sleep, my mate and I;
I," said the dove, from the rafters high.

And every beast, by some good spell,
In the stable dark was glad to tell
Of the gift he gave Immanuel;
The gift he gave Immanuel.[56]

---

56. Coffin, *Prince of Peace*,

THE POETRY OF CHRISTMAS

Robert Davis (1881–1950).

Based on *Orientis Partibus*, a twelfth-century song attributed to Pierre de Corbeil, Bishop of Sens, France, and recorded by many artists including Burl Ives and Johnny Cash.

Guided Tour

"Welcome to our authentic reconstruction
of a carpenter's workshop.
Notice the authentic crib (or manger)—
fully sanitized—
visitors disliked the odor. . .

"This wooden object
is a replica plow-share;
it should have a blade
but metal's requisitioned—
the war effort, you understand...

"That's an alabaster casket
(our one's *ersatz*—
funds don't stretch. . .).
Careful—it's quite fragile!

"On your way out—for me?
How kind! Don't miss
the mini-crosses:
inexpensive, thickly varnished
—so no risk of splinters."

Tim Dowley (1946–).

It Happened on Christmas Day

800	Pope Leo III crowned Charlemagne Holy Roman Emperor.
1066	William the Conqueror crowned in Westminster Abbey, London.
1492	Columbus' ship *Santa Maria* sank on Hispaniola.
1559	City of Natal founded, Brazil.
1643	Christmas Island discovered and named.
1776	George Washington crossed Delaware River with Continental Army.
1914	Unofficial truce in parts of the Western Front, World War I.
1926	Emperor Hirohito assumed Japanese throne.
1989	Nicolae Ceausescu executed in Romania.
1990	First communication on world-wide web.
1991	Mikhail Gorbachev resigned as President of USSR

CHRISTMAS DAY DEMISE

1946   W. C. Fields, American writer and comedian.

1963   Tristan Tzara, Romanian/French poet.

1977   Charlie Chaplin, English actor.

1983   Joan Miró, Spanish painter.

1992   Helen Joseph, South African anti-apartheid campaigner.

1995   Dean Martin, American swing singer.

2006   James Brown, American singer.

2008   Eartha Kitt, American singer.

2016   George Michael, English singer.

*Dickensian Christmases—
and others*

A Lover's Complaint

Mr. SPECTATOR,

I am a young Woman, and have my Fortune to make, for which Reason I come constantly to Church to hear divine Service, and make Conquests; but one great Hindrance in this my Design is, that our Clerk, who was once a Gardener, has this Christmas so over-decked the Church with Greens, that he has quite spoil'd my Prospect, insomuch that I have scarce seen the young Baronet I dress at these three Weeks, though we have both been very Constant at our Devotions, and do not sit above three Pews off. The Church, as it is now equipped, looks more like a Green-house than a Place of Worship; the middle Isle is a very pretty Shady Walk, and the Pews look like so many Arbours on each Side of it. The Pulpit itself has such Clusters of Ivy, Holly, and Rosemary about it, that a light Fellow in our Pew took Occasion to say, that the Congregation heard the Word out of a Bush, like *Moses*. Sir *Anthony Love's* Pew in particular is so well hedg'd, that all my Batteries have no Effect. I am obliged to shoot at Random among the Boughs, without taking any Manner of Aim. Mr. *Spectator*, unless you will give Orders for removing these Greens, I shall grow a very aukward Creature at Church, and soon have little Else to do there but say my Prayers. I am in Haste,
Dear Sir,
Your most obedient Servant,
Jenny Simper.[57]

Fictional letter published in *The Spectator*, December 1767, London.

---

57. Lewis, *Christmas*, p. 21.

Christmas with Sir Roger

. . .Sir *Roger*, after the laudable Custom of his Ancestors, always keeps open House at Christmas. I learned from him that he had killed eight Fat Hogs for the season . . . and that in particular he had sent a String of Hogs'-puddings with a Pack of Cards to every poor Family in the Parish. I have often thought, says Sir *Roger*, it happens very well that Christmas should fall out in the Middle of Winter. It is the most dead uncomfortable Time of the Year, when the poor People would suffer very much from their Poverty and Cold, if they had not good Chear, warm Fires, and Christmas Gambols to support them. I love to rejoice their poor Hearts at this Season, and to see the whole Village merry in my great Hall. I allow a double Quantity of Malt to my Small Beer, and set it a-running for twelve Days to everyone that calls for it. I have always a Piece of Cold Beef and a Mince-pye upon the Table, and am wonderfully pleased to see my Tenants pass away a whole Evening in playing their innocent Tricks, and smutting one another . . .[58]

Joseph Addison, in *The Spectator* No. 269.
Sir Roger de Coverley was a lovable, slightly ridiculous, character created by Joseph Addison and Richard Steele to exemplify the values of an elderly country gentleman in the time of Queen Anne.

58. Lewis, *Christmas*, p. 88.

Christmas Time

Christmas time! That man must be a misanthrope indeed, in whose breast something like a jovial feeling is not roused—in whose mind some pleasant associations are not awakened—by the recurrence of Christmas. There are people who will tell you that Christmas is not to them what it used to be; that each succeeding Christmas has found some cherished hope, or happy prospect, of the year before, dimmed or passed away; that the present only serves to remind them of reduced circumstances and straitened incomes—of the feasts they once bestowed on hollow friends, and of the cold looks that meet them now, in adversity and misfortune. Never heed such dismal reminiscences.. . .

Who can be insensible to the outpourings of good feeling, and the honest interchange of affectionate attachment, which abound at this season of the year? A Christmas family-party! We know nothing in nature more delightful! There seems a magic in the very name of Christmas. Petty jealousies and discords are forgotten; social feelings are awakened, in bosoms to which they have long been strangers; father and son, or brother and sister, who have met and passed with averted gaze, or a look of cold recognition, for months before, proffer and return the cordial embrace, and bury their past animosities in their present happiness. Kindly hearts that have yearned towards each other but have been withheld by false notions of pride and self-dignity, are again reunited, and all is kindness and benevolence! Would that Christmas lasted the whole year through . . .[59]

From *Sketches by Boz*, Charles Dickens, 1836.
Since Dickens more or less invented the Victorian Christmas, we have included a number of extracts from his work.

59. Dickens, *Boz*, pp. 258-9.

A Dickensian Christmas

As to the dinner, it's perfectly delightful—nothing goes wrong, and everybody is in the very best of spirits, and disposed to please and be pleased. Grandpapa relates a circumstantial account of the purchase of the turkey, with a slight digression relative to the purchase of previous turkeys, on former Christmas-days, which grandmamma corroborates in the minutest particular. Uncle George tells stories, and carves poultry, and takes wine, and jokes with the children at the side table, and winks at the cousins that are making love, or being made love to, and exhilarates everybody with his good humour and hospitality; and when, at last, a stout servant staggers in with a gigantic pudding, with a sprig of holly in the top, there is such a laughing, and shouting, and clapping of little chubby hands, and kicking up of fat dumpy legs, as can only be equalled by the applause with which the astonishing feat of pouring lighted brandy into mince-pies is received by the younger visitors. Then the dessert!—and the wine!—and the fun! Such beautiful speeches, and *such* songs, from aunt Margaret's husband, who turns out to be such a nice man, and *so* attentive to grandmamma! Even grandpapa not only sings his annual song with unprecedented vigour, but on being honoured with an unanimous *encore*, according to annual custom, actually comes out with a new one which nobody but grandmamma ever heard before; and a young scape-grace of a cousin, who has been in some disgrace with the old people, for certain heinous sins of omission and commission—neglecting to call, and persisting in drinking Burton Ale—astonishes everybody into convulsions of laughter by volunteering the most extraordinary comic songs that ever were heard. And thus the evening passes, in a strain of rational good will and cheerfulness, doing more to awaken the sympathies of every member of the party in behalf of his neighbour, and to perpetuate their good feeling during the ensuing year, than half the homilies that have ever been written, by half the Divines that have ever lived.[60]

Charles Dickens, from *Sketches by Boz*.

60. Slater, *Boz*, p. 219.

Christmas Afternoon: Done in the Manner, if not the Spirit, of Dickens

What an afternoon! Mr Gummidge said that, in his estimation, there never had been such an afternoon since the world began, a sentiment which was heartily endorsed by Mrs Gummidge and all the little Gummidges, not to mention the relatives who had come over from Jersey for the day.

In the first place, there was the ennui. And such ennui as it was! A heavy, overpowering ennui, such as results from a participation in eight courses of steaming, gravied food, topping off with salted nuts which the little old spinster Gummidge from Oak Hill said she never knew when to stop eating—and true enough she didn't—a dragging, devitalizing ennui, which left its victims strewn about the living-room in various attitudes of prostration suggestive of those of the petrified occupants in a newly unearthed Pompeiian dwelling; an ennui which carried with it a retinue of yawns, snarls and thinly veiled insults, and which ended in ruptures in the clan spirit serious enough to last throughout the glad new year.

Then there were the toys! Three and a quarter dozen toys to be divided among seven children. Surely enough, you or I might say, to satisfy the little tots. But that would be because we didn't know the tots. In came Baby Lester Gummidge, Lillian's boy, dragging an electric grain-elevator which happened to be the only toy in the entire collection which appealed to little Norman, five-year-old son of Luther, who lived in Rahway. In came curly-headed Effie in frantic and throaty disputation with Arthur, Jr., over the possession of an articulated zebra... In they all came, one after another, some crying, some snapping, some pulling, some pushing—all appealing to their respective parents for aid in their intra-mural warfare.

And the cigar smoke! Mrs Gummidge said that she didn't mind the smoke from a good cigarette, but would they mind if she opened the windows for just a minute in order to clear the room of the heavy aroma of used cigars? Mr Gummidge stoutly maintained that they were good cigars. His brother, George Gummidge, said that he, likewise, would say that they were. At which colloquial sally both the Gummidge brothers laughed testily, thereby breaking the laughter record for the afternoon . . .

. . .[F]inally Mrs Gummidge passed the Christmas candy around. Mr Gummidge afterward admitted that this was a tactical error on the part of his spouse. I no more believe that Mrs Gummidge thought they wanted that Christmas candy than I believe that she thought they wanted the cold turkey which she later suggested. My opinion is that she wanted to drive them home. At any rate, that is what she succeeded in doing. Such cries as there were of "Ugh! Don't let me see another thing to eat!" and "Take it away!" Then came hurried scramblings in the coat-closet for overshoes. There were the rasping sounds made by cross parents when putting wraps on children. There were insincere exhortations to "come and see us soon" and to "get together for lunch some time". And, finally, there were slammings of doors and the silence of utter exhaustion, while Mrs Gummidge went about picking up stray sheets of wrapping paper.

And, as Tiny Tim might say in speaking of Christmas afternoon as an institution, "God help us, everyone."[61]

Robert Benchley (1889–1945), American humorist.

---

61. Brandreth, *Christmas*, pp. 35–39.

Christmas with the Gargerys

Mr. Wopsle, the clerk at church, was to dine with us; and Mr. Hubble, the wheelwright, and Mrs. Hubble; and Uncle Pumblechook ... who was a well-to-do corn-chandler in the nearest town, and drove his own chaise-cart. The dinner hour was half-past one. When Joe and I got home, we found the table laid, and Mrs. Joe dressed, and the dinner dressing, and the front door unlocked (it never was at any other time) for the company to enter by, and everything most splendid ...

"Mrs. Joe," said Uncle Pumblechook; a large hard-breathing middle-aged slow man, with a mouth like a fish, dull staring eyes, and sandy hair standing upright on his head, so that he looked as if he had just been all but choked, and had that moment come to. "I have brought you as the compliments of the season—I have brought you, Mum, a bottle of sherry wine—and I have brought you, Mum, a bottle of port wine."

Every Christmas Day he presented himself, as a profound novelty, with exactly the same words, and carrying the two bottles like dumb-bells. Every Christmas Day, Mrs. Joe replied, as she now replied, "Oh, Un—cle Pum—ble—chook! This is kind!" Every Christmas Day, he retorted, as he now retorted, "It's no more than your merits. And now are you all bobbish, and how's Sixpennorth of halfpence?" meaning me.[62]

Charles Dickens, *Great Expectations*.

---

62. Dickens, *Great Expectations*, p. 21.

Bah! Humbug!

The door of Scrooge's counting-house was open that he might keep his eye upon his clerk, who in a dismal little cell beyond, a sort of tank, was copying letters. Scrooge had a very small fire, but the clerk's fire was so very much smaller that it looked like one coal. But he couldn't replenish it, for Scrooge kept the coal-box in his own room... Wherefore the clerk put on his white comforter, and tried to warm himself at the candle; in which effort, not being a man of a strong imagination, he failed.

"A merry Christmas, uncle! God save you!" cried a cheerful voice. It was the voice of Scrooge's nephew, who came upon him so quickly that this was the first intimation he had of his approach.

"Bah!" said Scrooge, "Humbug!"

He had so heated himself with rapid walking in the fog and frost, this nephew of Scrooge's, that he was all in a glow; his face was ruddy and handsome; his eyes sparkled, and his breath smoked again.

"Christmas a humbug, uncle!" said Scrooge's nephew. "You don't mean that, I am sure?"

"I do," said Scrooge. "Merry Christmas! What right have you to be merry? What reason have you to be merry? You're poor enough."

"Come, then," returned the nephew gaily. "What right have you to be dismal? What reason have you to be morose? You're rich enough."

Scrooge having no better answer ready on the spur of the moment, said, "Bah!" again; and followed it up with "Humbug."

"Don't be cross, uncle!" said the nephew.

"What else can I be," returned the uncle, "when I live in such a world of fools as this? Merry Christmas! Out upon merry Christmas! . . ."[63]

Charles Dickens: *A Christmas Carol*, 1843.

63. Dickens, *Christmas Carol*, p. 5.

"Marley's Ghost", illustration by John Leech from *A Christmas Carol*, 1843.

The Cratchits' Christmas

At last the dishes were set on, and grace was said. It was succeeded by a breathless pause, as Mrs Cratchit, looking slowly all along the carving-knife, prepared to plunge it in the breast; but when she did, and when the long expected gush of stuffing issued forth, one murmur of delight arose all round the board, and even Tiny Tim, excited by the two young Cratchits, beat on the table with the handle of his knife, and feebly cried Hurrah![64]

Charles Dickens, *A Christmas Carol.*

64. Dickens, *Christmas Carol*, p. 49.

Publishing Scrooge

Dickens originally published *A Christmas Carol* on 19 December 1843; since then, it has never been out of print. It was based partly on a story in *The Pickwick Papers,* in which an old sexton named Gabriel Grub is converted from his misanthropy by visits from goblins; some claim Dickens was also influenced by Jesus' parable of the rich fool in Luke 12:13–21.

Unusually, Dickens paid for the story's publication. The book was expensive to produce, as it included hand-colored illustrations and gilt-edged pages. However the first print-run of 6,000 sold out by Christmas Eve.

Christmas at the Mill on the Floss

And yet this Christmas day, in spite of Tom's fresh delight in home, was not, he thought, somehow or other, quite so happy as it had always been before. The red berries were just as abundant on the holly, and he and Maggie had dressed all the windows and mantelpieces and picture-frames on Christmas Eve with as much taste as ever, wedding the thick-set scarlet clusters with branches of the black-berried ivy. There had been singing under the windows after midnight—supernatural singing, Maggie always felt, in spite of Tom's contemptuous insistence that the singers were old Patch, the parish clerk, and the rest of the church choir: she trembled with awe when their caroling broke in upon her dreams, and the image of men in fustian clothes was always thrust away by the vision of angels resting on the parted cloud. But the midnight chant had helped as usual to lift the morning above the level of common days; and then, there was the smell of hot toast and ale from the kitchen, at the breakfast hour; the favourite anthem, the green boughs and the short sermon, gave the appropriate festal character to the church-going; and aunt and uncle Moss, with all their seven children, were looking like so many reflectors of the bright parlour-fire, when the church-goers came back stamping the snow from their feet; the plum-pudding was of the same handsome round-ness as ever, and came in with the symbolic blue flames around it, as if it had been heroically snatched from the nether fires into which it had been thrown by dyspeptic puritans; the dessert was as splendid as ever with its golden oranges, brown nuts, and the crystalline light and dark of apple jelly and damson cheese: in all these things Christmas was as it had always been since Tom could remember; it was only distinguished, if by anything, by superior sliding and snowballs.[65]

George Eliot (1819–1880), English novelist.

65. Eliot, *Mill*, p.224.

Christmas at Noningsby

I do not know of anything more pleasant to the eye than a pretty country church, decorated for Christmas day. . . . [H]ere at Noningsby church, the winter flowers had been cut by Madeline and the gardener, and the red berries had been grouped by her own hands. She and the vicar's wife had stood together with perilous audacity on the top of the clerk's desk while they fixed the branches beneath the cushion of the old-fashioned turret, from which the sermons were preached . . . And the children had regarded the operation as a triumph of all that was wonderful in decoration; and thus many of them had been made happy.[66]

Anthony Trollope (1815–1882), English novelist.

66. Trollope, *Orley*, p. 195.

The Trouble with Clarinets

"Clar'nets, however, be bad at all times," said Michael Mail. "One Christmas—years agone now, years—I went the rounds wi' the Weatherbury quire. 'Twas a hard frosty night, and the keys of all the clar'nets froze—ah, they did freeze!—so that 'twas like drawing a cork every time a key was opened; the players o' 'em had to go into a hedger-and-ditcher's chimley-corner, and thaw their clar'nets every now and then. An icicle o' spet hung down from the end of every man's clar'net a span long; and as to fingers—well, there, if ye'll believe me, we had no fingers at all, to our knowing."

"I can well bring back to my mind," said Mr. Penny, "what I said to poor Joseph Ryme (who took the treble part in Chalk-Newton Church for two-and-forty year) when they thought of having clar'nets there. 'Joseph,' I said says I, 'depend upon't, if so be you have them tooting clar'nets you'll spoil the whole set-out. Clar'nets were not made for the service of the Lard; you can see it by looking at 'em,' I said. And what came o't? Why, souls, the parson set up a barrel-organ on his own account within two years o' the time I spoke, and the old quire went to nothing."

"As far as look is concerned," said the tranter, "I don't for my part see that a fiddle is much nearer heaven than a clar'net. 'Tis farther off. There's always a rakish, scampish twist about a fiddle's looks that seems to say the Wicked One had a hand in making o'en; while angels be supposed to play clar'nets in heaven, or som'at like 'em, if ye may believe picters."[67]

Thomas Hardy (1840–1928).

---

67. Hardy, *Greenwood*, p. 25.

Christmas Night

But it is in the old story that all the beasts can talk, in the night between Christmas Eve and Christmas Day in the morning (though there are very few folk that can hear them, or know what it is that they say).

When the Cathedral clock struck twelve there was an answer—like an echo of the chimes—and Simpkin heard it, and came out of the tailor's door, and wandered about in the snow.

From all the roofs and gables and old wooden houses in Gloucester came a thousand merry voices singing the old Christmas rhymes—all the old songs that ever I heard of, and some that I don't know; like Whittington's bells.

First and loudest the cocks cried out—"Dame, get up, and bake your pies!"

"Oh, dilly, dilly, dilly!" sighed Simpkin.

And now in a garret there were lights and sounds of dancing, and cats came from over the way.

"Hey, diddle, diddle, the cat and the fiddle! All the cats in Gloucester—except me," said Simpkin.

Under the wooden eaves the starlings and sparrows sang of Christmas pies; the jack-daws woke up in the Cathedral tower; and although it was the middle of the night the throstles and robins sang; the air was quite full of little twittering tunes.[68]

Beatrix Potter (1866–1943), English writer and artist.

---

68. Potter, *Gloucester*, pp. 52, 57.

Field-mice Carolers

"What's up?" inquired the Rat, pausing in his labours.

"I think it must be the field-mice," replied the Mole, with a touch of pride in his manner. "They go round carol-singing regularly at this time of the year. They're quite an institution in these parts. And they never pass me over—they come to Mole End last of all; and I used to give them hot drinks, and supper too sometimes, when I could afford it. It will be like old times to hear them again."

"Let's have a look at them!" cried the Rat, jumping up and running to the door.

It was a pretty sight, and a seasonable one, that met their eyes when they flung the door open. In the fore-court, lit by the dim rays of a horn lantern, some eight or ten little field-mice stood in a semicircle, red worsted comforters round their throats, their fore-paws thrust deep into their pockets, their feet jigging for warmth. With bright beady eyes they glanced shyly at each other, sniggering a little, sniffing and applying coat-sleeves a good deal. As the door opened, one of the elder ones that carried the lantern was just saying, "Now then, one, two, three!" and forthwith their shrill little voices uprose on the air, singing one of the old-time carols that their forefathers composed in fields that were fallow and held by frost, or when snow-bound in chimney corners, and handed down to be sung in the miry street to lamp-lit windows at Yule-time.[69]

Kenneth Grahame (1859–1932), British writer.

---

69. Grahame, *Willows*, pp. 93–95.

Home for Christmas

Everybody was mad with excitement. William was coming on Christmas Eve. Mrs. Morel surveyed her pantry. There was a big plum cake, and a rice cake; jam tarts, lemon tarts, and mince pies, two enormous dishes. She was finishing cooking—Spanish tarts and cheese-cakes. Everywhere was decorated. The kissing-bunch of berried holly hung with bright and glittering things, spun slowly over Mrs. Morel's head as she trimmed her little tarts in the kitchen. A great fire roared. There was a scent of cooked pastry. He was due at seven o'clock, but he would be late. The three children had gone to meet him. She was alone. But at a quarter to seven Morel came in again. Neither wife nor husband spoke. He sat in his arm-chair, quite awkward with excitement, and she quietly went on with her baking. Only by the careful way in which she did things could it be told how much moved she was. The clock ticked on.

"What time dost say he's coming?" Morel asked, for the fifth time.

"The train gets in at half-past six," she replied, emphatically.

"Then he'll be here at ten past seven." . . .

The kettle was singing. They waited and waited.[70]

D. H. Lawrence (1885–1930), English novelist.

---

70. Lawrence, *Lovers*, p. 104.

Waiting

The expectation grew more tense. The star was risen into the sky, the songs, the carols were ready to hail it. The star was the sign in the sky. Earth too should give a sign. As evening drew on, hearts beat fast with anticipation, hands were full of ready gifts. There were the tremulously expectant words of the church service, the night was past and the morning was come, the gifts were given and received, joy and peace made a flapping of wings in each heart, there was a great burst of carols, the Peace of the World had dawned, strife had passed away, every hand was linked in hand, every heart was singing.[71]

D. H. Lawrence.

71. Lawrence, *Rainbow*, p. 260.

Seven Times a Week

This brings me to the second fallacy. I refer to the belief that "Christmas comes but once a year." Perhaps it does, according to the calendar—a quaint and interesting compilation, but of little or no practical value to anybody... Spiritually, Christmas Day recurs exactly seven times a week. When we have frankly acknowledged this, and acted on this, we shall begin to realize the Day's mystical and terrific beauty. For it is only every-day things that reveal themselves to us in all their wonder and their splendour. A man who happens one day to be knocked down by a motor-bus merely utters a curse and instructs his solicitor; but a man who has been knocked down by a motor-bus every day of the year will have begun to feel that he is taking part in an august and soul-cleansing ritual . . .

I look for the time when we shall wish one another a Merry Christmas every morning; when roast turkey and plum-pudding shall be the staple of our daily dinner, and the holly shall never be taken down from the walls, and everyone will always be kissing everyone else under the mistletoe . . .[72]

Max Beerbohm (1872–1956), English essayist, parodying the paradoxical style of G. K. Chesterton.

72. Beerbohm, *Christmas Garland*, pp. 51–52.

"Christmas crackers", illustration by Christian Wilhelm Allers, 1888.

Christmas at Cold Comfort Farm

It was Christmas Eve. Dusk, a filthy mantle, lay over Sussex when the Reverend Silas Hearsay, Vicar of Howling, set out to pay his yearly visit to Cold Comfort Farm. Earlier in the afternoon he had feared he would not be Guided to go there, but then he had seen a crate of British Port-type wine go past the Vicarage on the grocer's boy's bicycle, and it could only be going, by that road, to the farmhouse. Shortly afterwards he was Guided to go, and set out upon his bicycle.

The Starkadders, of Cold Comfort Farm, had never got the hang of Christmas, somehow, and on Boxing Day there was always a run on the Howling Pharmacy for lint, bandages, and boracic powder. So the Vicar was going up there, as he did every year, to show them the ropes a bit . . .

After removing two large heaps of tussocks which blocked the lane leading to the Farm and thereby releasing a flood of muddy, icy water over his ankles, the Vicar wheeled his machine on towards the farmhouse, reflecting that those tussocks had never fallen there from the dung-cart of Nature. It was clear that someone did not want him to come to the place. He pushed his bicycle savagely up the hill, muttering.

The farmhouse was in silence and darkness. He pulled the ancient hell-bell (once used to warn excommunicated persons to stay away from Divine Service) hanging outside the front door, and waited.

For a goodish bit nothing happened. Suddenly a window far above his head was flung open and a voice wailed into the twilight—

"No! No! No!"

And the window slammed shut again.

"You're making a mistake, I'm sure," shouted the Vicar, peering up into the webby thongs of the darkness. "It's me. The Rev. Silas Hearsay."

There was a pause. Then—

"Beant you postman?" asked the voice, rather embarrassed . . .[73]

From Stella Gibbons (1902–1989), *Christmas at Cold Comfort Farm*, 1940. Sequel to *Cold Comfort Farm*, a parody of romanticized, doom-laden accounts of English country life.

73. Gibbons, *Christmas*, pp. 18–19.

MORE HOLIDAY HUMOR

Terrible Jokes

What does Father Christmas do when his elves misbehave?
He gives them the sack.

What did one Christmas tree say to the other?
I've got a present fir you.

What did Adam say the day before Christmas?
"It's Christmas, Eve."

What do vampires write in their Christmas cards?
Best vicious of the season.

Why is it hard to find an Advent Calendar?
Because their days are numbered.

Knock, knock!

Knock, knock.
Who's there?
Wendy.
Wendy who?
Wendy red, red robin comes bobbin' along.

Knock, knock.
Who's there?
Wayne.
Wayne who?
Wayne a manger.

Knock, knock.
Who's there?
Doughnut.
Doughnut who?
Doughnut open till Christmas.

Knock, knock.
Who's there?
Carol singers.
Do you know what time it is?
No—but if you hum it we'll sing it.

Santa

What do you call people who are afraid of Santa Claus?
Claustrophobic.

Why does Santa have three gardens?
So he can hoe, hoe, hoe.

If Santa Claus had a child what would it be called?
Subordinate Clause.

What did Mrs Claus say to Santa?
It looks like rain, dear.

What do you call someone who doesn't believe in Father Christmas?
A rebel without a Claus.

What did Santa say to his reindeer?
You sleigh me.

What's Santa's wife called?
Mary Christmas.

Why did Santa get a parking ticket?
Because he left his sleigh in a snow-parking zone.

Christmas in Church

Earthly and Eternal Kings

You well know what joy and what a gathering there is when the birthday of the emperor of this world is to be celebrated; how his generals and princes and soldiers, arrayed in silk garments and girt with precious belts worked with shining gold, seek to enter the king's presence in more brilliant fashion than usual.... If, therefore, brethren, those of this world celebrate the birthday of an earthly king with such an outlay for the sake of the glory of the present honor, with what solicitude ought we to celebrate the birthday of our eternal king Jesus Christ who in return for our devotion will bestow on us not temporal but eternal glory.

Maximus, Bishop of Turin, Italy (c. 350–c. 423).[74]

74. Ramsey, *Sermons*, p.14.

N OW E L L ! A C H R I S T M A S M I S C E L L A N Y

A Sermon preached before the King's Majesty, at Whitehall, on Wednesday, the Twenty-Fifth of December, A.D. MDCXXII, being Christmas-Day.

Behold there came wise men from the East to Jerusalem, saying, Where is the King of the Jews that is born? For we have seen his star in the East, and are come to worship Him (Matthew 2:1).

. . .Last we consider the time of their coming, the season of the year. It was no summer progress. A cold coming they had of it at this time of the year, just the worst time of the year to take a journey, and specially a long journey. The ways deep, the weather sharp, the days short, the sun farthest off . . . in "the very dead of winter" . . .

And these difficulties they overcame, of a wearisome, irksome, troublesome, dangerous, unseasonable journey; and for all this they came. And came it cheerfully and quickly, as appeared by the speed they made. It was but *vidimus, venimus,* with them; "they saw," and "they came"; no sooner saw, but they set out presently. So as upon the first appearing of the star (as it might be last night), they knew it was Balaam's star; it called them away, they made ready straight to begin their journey this morning . . .[75]

Lancelot Andrewes (1555–1626), Bishop of Winchester, preaching to King James I.
T. S. Eliot quoted from this sermon in his poem "The Journey of the Magi".

---

75. Howse, *Sermons*, p. 55.

Christmas Day, 1625

Christ had one privilege in his birth which never any prince had or shall have: that is, that he chose what mother he would have, and might have been born of what woman he would have chosen. And in this large and universal choice, though he chose a woman full of grace to be his mother, yet, that he might give spiritual comfort to all sorts of women—first to those who should be unjustly suspected and insimulated [charged] of sin and incontinency when indeed they were innocent—he was content to come of a mother who should be subject to that suspicion, and whom her husband should think to be with child before he married her and therefore purpose to put her away.

And then, to fill those women who had been guilty of that sin with relief in their consciences against the wrath of God, and with reparation of their reputation and good name in the world, it was his unsearchable will and pleasure that in all that genealogy and pedigree which he and his Spirit hath inspired the Evangelists to record of his ancestors, there is not one woman named of whom Christ is descended who is not dangerously noted in the Scriptures to have had some aspersion of incontinence upon her—as both St Jerome and St Ambrose and St Chrysostom observe of Tamar, of Bathsheba, and of Ruth also.

So then Christ Jesus, who came only for the relief of sinners, is content to be known to have come not only of poor parents but of a sinful race.[76]

John Donne (1571 or 1572–1631), English poet and Dean of St Paul's Cathedral, London.

76. Scott, *Donne*, p. 157.

Pepys at Christmas

25 December 1662

Up pretty early, leaving my wife not well in bed. And with my boy walked, it being a most brave cold and dry frosty morning, and had a pleasant walk to Whitehall; where I entended to have received the Communion with the family, but I came a little too late . . . By and by down to the Chappell again, where Bishop Morley preached upon the Song of the Angels—"Glory to God on high—on earth peace, and good will towards men." Methought he made but a poor sermon, but long and reprehending the mistaken jollity of the Court for the true joy that shall and ought to be on these days. Perticularized concerning their excess in playes and gameing... Upon which it was worth observing how far they are come from taking the Reprehensions of a Bishop seriously, that they all laugh in the chapel when he reflected on their ill actions and courses.

He did much press us to joy in these public days of joy, and to hospitality. But one that stood by whispered in my ear that the bishop himself do not spend one groat to the poor himself.

The sermon done, a good Anthemne followed, with vials; and the King came down to receive the Sacrament, but I stayed not; but calling my boy from my Lord's lodgings and giving Sarah some good advice, by my Lord's order, to be Sober, and look after the house, I walked home again with great pleasure; and there dined by my wife's bedside with great content, having a mess of brave plum-porridge and a roasted Pullet for dinner; and I sent for a mince-pie abroad, my wife not being well, to make any herself yet.[77]

Samuel Pepys (1633–1703), English diarist.

77. Pepys, *Diary*, p. 245.

A Good Sermon

Christmas Day, 1664.

Up (my wife's eye being ill still of the blow I did in a passion give her on Monday last) to church alone—where Mr. Mills, a good sermon. . . . After dinner . . . to Mr. Rawlinson's church, where I heard a good sermon of one that I remember was at Pauls[78] with me, his name Maggett. And very great store of fine women there is in this church, more than I know anywhere else about us.[79]

Samuel Pepys.

78. St Paul's Cathedral.
79. Pepys, *Diary*, p. 454.

TRADITIONS OF THE MAGI

Numerous myths and legends have arisen around the "wise men" (KJV) of Matthew 2.

By tradition known as the "Magi", they are also referred to as "Three Wise Men" and "Three Kings".

Magi is the plural of "magus", a member of a Persian priestly caste. The Bible never names the Magi, nor does it say how many there were. Matthew's Gospel lists three gifts—gold, frankincense, and myrrh—so it is often inferred there were three Magi.

The Magi are frequently named as Caspar, Melchior, and Balthasar. Other names include Larvandad, Hormisdad, and Gushnasaph. The Eastern Church claims there were twelve Magi.

Western Christian art depicts two, three, four—and as many as eight Magi.

The gifts of the Magi are often interpreted symbolically: gold representing Christ's kingship; frankincense—the purest incense—his divinity; myrrh—a medicine—his humanity.

The Magi followed the Star of Bethlehem to find Jesus. Some believe it was actually a comet; others, that it was a conjunction of the planets Jupiter and Saturn.

In the 1270s, the Venetian traveler Marco Polo claimed he had visited the tombs of the Magi, in the city of Saba, Persia.

Cologne Cathedral, Germany, claims it preserves the bones of the Magi.

Carols

Of a Rose, a Lovely Rose

Of a rose, a lovely rose,
Of a rose is al my song.

Lestenyt,[80] lordyngs, both elde and yinge,[81]
How this rose began to sprynge;
Swych a rose to myn lykynge
    In al this word[82] ne knowe I non.

The Aungil came fro hevene tour,
To grete Marye with gret honour,
And seyde sche xuld[83] bere the flour
    That xulde breke the fyndes bond.

The flour sprong in heye Bedlem,
That is bothe bryht and schen:[84]
The rose is Mary hevene qwyn,[85]
    Out of here bosum the blosme sprong.

The ferste braunche is ful of myht,
That sprang on Cyrstemesse nyht,
The sterre schon over Bedlem bryht
    That is bothe brod and long.

80. listen.
81. young.
82. world.
83. should.
84. beautiful.
85. heaven's queen.

The secunde braunche sprong to helle,
The fendys power doun to felle:
Therein myht non sowle dwelle;
    Blyssid be the time the rose sprong!

The thredde braunche is good and swote,
It sprang to hevene crop and rote,
Therein to dwellyn and ben our bote;[86]
    Every day it schewit in prystes hond.

Prey we to here with gret honour,
Che that bar the blyssid flowr,
Che be our helpe and our socour
    And schyd us fro the fyndes bond.[87]

English, fifteenth-century.
Anonymous.

---

86. salvation.
87. Quiller-Couch, *English Verse*, p. 9.

Welcome Yule

Welcome Yule, thou merry man,
In worship of this holy day!
Welcome be thou, heaven-king,
Welcome born in one morning,
Welcome for whom we shall sing,
Welcome Yule.

Welcome be ye, Stephen and John,
Welcome Innocents every one,
Welcome Thomas, Martyr one:

Welcome be ye, good New Year,
Welcome Twelfth Day both in fere;[88]
Welcome Saintès lief[89] and dear;

Welcome be ye, Candlemas,
Welcome be ye, queen of bliss,
Welcome both to more and less:

Welcome be ye that are here,
Welcome all, and make good cheer,
Welcome all another year![90]

English, fifteenth-century.
Anonymous.

88. together.
89. beloved.
90. Dearmer, *Carols*, p. 369.

Coventry Carol

Lully, lullah, thou little tiny child,
Bye bye, lully, lullay.
Thou little tiny child,
Bye bye, lully, lullay.

O sisters too, how may we do
For to preserve, this day,
This poor youngling for whom we sing,
"Bye bye, lully, lullay"?

Herod the king, in his raging,
Chargèd he hath this day
His men of might in his own sight
All young children to slay.

That woe is me, poor child, for thee
And ever mourn and may
For thy parting neither say nor sing,
"Bye bye, lully, lullay."[91]

From the *Pageant of the Shearmen and Tailors*, one of the
Coventry Mystery plays, c. 1534.

---

91. Lawson-Jones, *Partridge*, pp. 44–49.

My Dancing Day

To-morrow shall be my dancing day:
I would my true love did so chance
To see the legend of my play,
To call my true love to my dance:
Sing O my love, O my love, my love, my love;
This have I done for my true love.

Then was I born of a virgin pure,
Of her I took my fleshly substánce;
Thus was I knit to man's natúre,
To call my true love to my dance:

In a manger laid and wrapped I was,
So very poor, this was my chance,
Betwixt an ox and a silly[92] poor ass,
To call my true love to my dance.[93]

Anonymous.
Opening stanzas of a carol that may have originated in the sung
and danced ending to the first or second day of a three-day
Cornish religious drama.

---

92. helpless.
93. Dearmer, *Carols*, p. 155.

Noel, Noel, Noel

"Noel, noel, noel",
Sing we with mirth;
Christ is come well
With us to dwell
By His most noble birth.

Under a tree, in sporting me
Alone by a wood side,
I heard a maid that sweetly said
"I am with child this tide.

"Graciously conceived have I
The Son of God so sweet.
His gracious will I put me till
As mother him to keep.

"Both night and day I will Him pray
And hear his lawès taught,
And every deal His true gospel
In His apostles fraught.

"This ghostly case doth me embrace
Without despite or mock,
With my darling "lullay" to sing
And lovely Him to rock.

"Without distress, in great lightness
I am both night and day:
This heavenly Fode in His childhood
Shall daily with me play.

"Soon must I sing with rejoicing,
For the time is all run
That I shall child, all undefiled,
The King of heaven's Son."[94]

English, fifteenth century.
Anonymous.

94. Brooks-Davies, *Christmas Please!*, p. 36.

Sing We Yule

Make we mirth
For Christes birth,
And sing we Yole till Candlemess.

The first day of Yole have we in mind
How God was man born of our kind,[95]
For he the bondes wold unbind
Of all our sinnes and wickedness.

The second day we sing of Stephen,
Who stoned was and steyed up even[96]
To God that he saw stond in Heven,
And crowned was for his prowess.

The third day longeth[97] to Sent John,
Who was Christes darling, derer non:
Whom he betok, whan he shuld gon,
His moder der for her clenness.[98]

The fourth day of the children yong,
That Herowd to deth had do[99] with wrong.
Of Christ they could non tell with tong,
But with their blod bore him witness.

95. nature.
96. ascended direct.
97. belongs.
98. to whom, when he had to go, he entrusted his mother for her purity.
99. put.

The fifth day longeth to Sent Thomas,
That as a strong pillar of bras
Held up the Chirch and slain he was,
For he stod with rightwesness.[100]

The eighth day Jesu took his name,
Who saved mankind fro sin and shame,
And circumcised was for no blame,
But for ensample of mekness.

The twelfth day offered to him kinges three
Gold, myrrh, and cence,[101] thes giftes free:[102]
For God, and man and King was he,
Thus worshipped they his worthiness.

On the fortieth day cam Mary mild
Unto the temple with her child
To shew her clen that never was filed,[103]
And therwith endeth Christmes.[104]

English, fifteenth-century.
Anonymous.

---

100. righteousness.
101. incense.
102. noble.
103. defiled.
104. Davies, *English Lyrics*, p. 167.

On Christmas Day

On Christmas Day it happened so
Down in the meadows for to plough
As he was a-ploughing on so fast
Up came Sweet Jesus Himself at last.

"O man, O man, what makes you plough
So hard upon the Lord's Birthday?"
The farmer answered Him with speed,
 "For the plough this day I have great need."

His arms did quaver to and fro,
His arms did quaver, he could not plough,
Fore the ground did open and let him in
Before he could repent of sin.

His wife and children [were] out of place,
His beasts and cattle were almost lost,
His beasts and cattle they died away,
For the breaking of our Lord's Birthday.[105]

An unusual image of a vengeful Jesus. A traditional carol
collected at Weobley, Herefordshire, England, from Esther Smith
by Ella Mary Leather and English composer Ralph Vaughan
Williams (1872–1958) in September 1913.

---

105. Leather, *Folklore*, p. 297.

Carol for Candlemas Day[106]

Christmas hath made an end,
Well-a-day! Well-a-day!
Which was my dearest friend,
More is the pity!
For with an heavy heart
Must I from thee depart,
To follow plow and cart
All the year after.

Lent is fast coming on,
That loves not anyone,
For I doubt both my cheeks
Will look thin eating leeks;
Wise is he then that seeks
For a friend in a corner.

All our good cheer is gone,
And turned to a bone,
In my good master's house
I shall eat no more souse,[107]
Then give me one carouse,
Gentle, kind butler!

106. Candlemas, 2 February, marked the conclusion of Christmas festivities.
107. Pickled meat or fish.

It grieves me to the heart,
From my friend to depart,
Christmas, I fear, 'tis thee
That thus forsaketh me:
Yet till one hour I see,
Will I be merry.[108]

Anonymous.

108. Bullen, *Garland*, p. 244.

A Sunny Bank

As I sat on a sunny bank,
On Christmas day in the morning.

I spied three ships come sailing by,
On Christmas day in the morning.

And who should be with those three ships
But Joseph and his fair lady!

O he did whistle, and she did sing,
On Christmas day in the morning.

And all the bells on earth did ring
On Christmas day in the morning.

For joy that our Savior Christ was born
On Christmas day in the morning.[109]

Anonymous.

109. Dearmer, *Carols*, p. 7.

Joseph and the Angel[110]

As Joseph was a-walking, he heard an angel sing:
"This night shall be bornèd our heavenly King.

"He neither shall be bornèd in housen nor in hall,
Nor in the place of paradise, but in an ox's stall.

"He neither shall be clothèd in purple nor in pall,
But in thew fair white linen, as usen babies all.

"He neither shall be rockèd in silver nor in gold,
But in a wooden cradle that rocks upon the mould.[111]

"He neither shall be christenèd in white wine nor red,
But with the fair spring water with which we were christenèd."[112]

English traditional.

110. "The Cherry Tree, Part II".
111. ground.
112. Keyte, *Carols*, p. 212.

Child in the Manger

Child in the manger, infant of Mary;
Outcast and stranger, Lord of all!
Child who inherits all our transgressions,
All our demerits on him fall.

Once the most holy child of salvation
Gentle and lowly lived below;
Now as our glorious mighty redeemer,
See him victorious o'er each foe.

Prophets foretold him, infant of wonder;
Angels behold him on his throne;
Worthy our Savior of all their praises;
Happy forever are his own.[113]

Mary Macdonald (1789–1872), translated from the original Gaelic
by Lachlan Macbean (1853–1931).[114]

113. *Hymns of Faith*, # 161.

114. Generally sung to the Gaelic tune "Bunessan", familiar as the setting
for "Morning has broken".

The Shepherds' Farewell

Thou must leave thy lowly dwelling,
The humble crib, the stable bare,
Babe, all mortal babes excelling,
Content our earthly lot to share,
Loving father, loving mother,
Shelter thee with tender care!

Blessèd Jesus, we implore thee
With humble love and holy fear,
In the land that lies before thee,
Forget not us who linger here!
May the shepherd's lowly calling
Ever to thy heart be dear!

Blest are ye beyond all measure,
Thou happy father, mother mild!
Guard ye well your heav'nly treasure,
The Prince of Peace, the Holy Child!
God go with you, God protect you,
Guide you safely through the wild![115]

Hector Berlioz (1803–1869), from his oratorio *L'enfance du Christ*.
Translated by Paul England (c. 1863–1932).

115. Jacques, *Carols*, p. 142.

Good King Wenceslas Looked Out

Good King Wenceslas looked out
On the feast of Stephen,
When the snow lay round about,
Deep and crisp and even;
Brightly shone the moon that night,
Though the frost was cruel,
When a poor man came in sight,
Gath'ring winter fuel.

"Hither, page, and stand by me;
If thou know'st it, telling—
Yonder peasant, who is he?
Where and what his dwelling?"
"Sire, he lives a good league hence,
Underneath the mountain,
Right against the forest fence,
By Saint Agnes' fountain."

"Bring me flesh, and bring me wine!
Bring me pine logs hither!
Thou and I shall see him dine
When we bear them thither."
Page and monarch, forth they went,
Forth they went together,
Through the rude wind's wild lament
And the bitter weather.

"Sire, the night is darker now,
And the wind blows stronger;
Fails my heart, I know not how;
I can go no longer."
"Mark my footsteps, good my page,
Tread thou in them boldly:
Thou shalt find the winter's rage
Freeze thy blood less coldly."

In his master's steps he trod,
Where the snow lay dinted;
Heat was in the very sod
Which the saint had printed.
Therefore, Christian men, be sure,
Wealth or rank possessing,
Ye who now will bless the poor,
Shall yourselves find blessing.[116]

John Mason Neale (1818–1866), English hymnwriter and translator.
Written to fit the thirteenth-century spring carol "*Tempus adest floridum*".

116. Keyte, *Carols*, p. 212.

Silent Night

Translated into any number of languages, "Silent Night" is sung by millions every Christmas. It is the most popular Christmas song in history, with more than 733 different versions copyrighted since 1978 and at least 137,000 known recordings. *"Heilige Nacht"* ("Silent Night") was probably first performed two centuries ago on Christmas Eve, 1818, at St Nicholas Church, Oberndorf, Lower Austria, during midnight mass. The village priest, Joseph Mohr, wrote the lyrics, his friend Franz Gruber (1787–1863), a school-teacher in nearby Arnsdorf, the melody, with the lilt of an Austrian folk-tune.

Possibly because of the carol's moving simplicity, many legends have accumulated claiming to explain its origin. One tale has mice destroying the bellows of the church organ, necessitating a new hymn which could be accompanied on a guitar. *Silent Mouse*, a 1988 television drama-doc narrated by Lynn Redgrave, recounted this story from the mouse's viewpoint. Another tale has the village priest penning last-minute lyrics, having discovered the organ was out of action. One version of this story adds that the instrument couldn't be repaired until the snows melted and spring arrived. An Austrian TV version of the tale shifts Oberndorf to the more photogenic Austrian Alps and adds to the cast villainous railway speculators and a two-faced priest; while a German writer gives Franz Gruber a zither rather than a guitar—and links the priest, Joseph Mohr, to a house fire in Salzburg. As for the melody, alternative composers proposed include Haydn, Mozart, and Beethoven. However, in 1995 a manuscript in Mohr's hand was discovered, with the inscription *"Melody of Father Xavier Gruber"*, definitively validating the Gruber/Mohr authorship.

Soon after the original performance of "Silent Night", a local organ-repairer named Karl Mauracher apparently found a copy of the carol at St. Nicholas Church which he took back to his native Ziller Valley. Two local families of itinerant folk-singers—similar to the Trapp Family Singers of *Sound of Music* fame—then added the song to their repertoire and trekked it around German-speaking countries. In 1839 the Rainer Family took *Stille Nacht* to America, performing it at the Alexander Hamilton Monument in the graveyard of New York's Trinity Church. The rector, John Freeman Young (1820–1885), created the now-familiar English version, "Silent Night".

The Twelve Days of Christmas

On the first day of Christmas my true love sent to me
A partridge in a pear tree.

On the second day of Christmas my true love sent to me
Two turtle doves,
And a partridge in a pear tree.

On the third day of Christmas my true love sent to me
Three French hens,
Two turtle doves,
And a partridge in a pear tree.

On the fourth day of Christmas my true love sent to me
Four cally[117] birds,
Three French hens (etc.)

On the fifth day of Christmas my true love sent to me
Five gold rings,
Four cally birds (etc.)

On the sixth day of Christmas my true love sent to me
Six geese a-laying,
Five gold rings (etc.)

On the seventh day of Christmas my true love sent to me
Seven swans a-swimming,
Six geese a laying (etc.)

On the eighth day of Christmas my true love sent to me
Eight maids a-milking,
Seven swans a-swimming (etc.)

117. Or "colly"—blackbird.

On the ninth day of Christmas my true love sent to me
Nine ladies dancing,
Eight maids a-milking (etc.)

On the tenth day of Christmas my true love sent to me
Ten lords a-leaping,
Nine ladies dancing (etc.)

On the eleventh day of Christmas my true love sent to me
Eleven pipers piping,
Ten lords a-leaping (etc.)

On the twelfth day of Christmas my true love sent to me
Twelve drummers drumming,
Eleven pipers piping (etc.)[118]

English traditional.

118. Keyte, *Carols*, p. 228.

Twelve Days

"The Twelve Days of Christmas" may not have the gravitas of "Once in Royal David's City", the poignancy of "In the Bleak Midwinter", or the rousing energy of "O Come, All Ye Faithful", but is sung as often as any of them. A Victorian pedant criticized "the utter absurdity of the words' and the lengthy carol perhaps outstays its welcome, yet it surely captures the festive spirit. There are dozens of recorded versions—from Burl Ives and the Vienna Boys' Choir to John Denver and the Muppets. Even Frank Sinatra had his turn, though he changed the familiar lines to "three golf clubs, two silken scarfs, and a most lovely lavender tie".

The carol first appeared in print around 1780 in a collection of children's verse called *Mirth without Mischief*. The "twelve days" are possibly rooted in the pagan midwinter festival of Yule, linked to the Norse god Odin. The church adopted a similar pattern, with Christmastide running from 25 December though 5 January—"Twelfth Night"—a period crammed with feasting and merry-making to ward off winter gloom and welcome the New Year. The musical arrangement used today is by Frederic Austin (1872–1952), who added the vital four-beat pause at "five gold rings".

Some have suggested the items listed in the carol represent wedding presents, with the partridge and the pear tree symbolizing sex and love. Others claim it was written in code during the Reformation to teach oppressed young Catholics their Catechism. By this interpretation the "three French hens" might represent the Trinity; the "four colly birds" the Gospels; the "lords-a-leaping" the Ten Commandments; and the "drummers drumming" the twelve disciples. A detailed key has been proposed—though it feels shoehorned in to prove a case:

131

NOWELL! A CHRISTMAS MISCELLANY

1. The partridge: a symbol of Christ. A mother partridge feigns injury to decoy predators from her nestlings, so giving her life for her children. The pear tree represents the cross.

2. Two turtle doves: the Old and New Testaments.

3. Three French hens: faith, hope, and charity (1 Corinthians 13:13).

4. Four colly birds: the four Gospels—Matthew, Mark, Luke, and John.

5. Five gold rings: The first five books of the Old Testament, the Torah—considered more valuable than gold by the Jews (Psalm 19:10).

6. Six geese a-laying: Eggs—symbols of new life.

7. Seven swans a-swimming: The seven gifts of the Holy Spirit—prophecy, service, teaching, encouragement, giving, leadership, and mercy (Romans 12:6-8).

8. Eight maids-a-milking: The eight Beatitudes (Matthew 5:3-10), which nourish like milk.

9. Nine ladies dancing: The nine fruits of the Holy Spirit: love, joy, peace, patience, kindness, goodness, faithfulness, gentleness, and self-control (Galatians 5:22-3).

10. Ten lords a-leaping: The Ten Commandments (Exodus 20:3-17).

11. Eleven pipers piping: The eleven apostles who remained loyal to Jesus.

12. Twelve drummers drumming: twelve core beliefs in the Apostles' Creed.

A Christmas Carol

In the bleak mid-winter
Frosty wind made moan,
Earth stood hard as iron,
Water like a stone;
Snow had fallen, snow on snow,
Snow on snow,
In the bleak mid-winter,
Long ago.

Our God, Heaven cannot hold Him
Nor earth sustain;
Heaven and earth shall flee away
When He comes to reign;
In the bleak mid-winter
A stable-place sufficed
The Lord God Almighty
Jesus Christ.

Enough for Him, whom cherubim
Worship night and day,
A breastful of milk
And a mangerful of hay;
Enough for Him, whom angels
Fall down before,
The ox and ass and camel
Which adore.

Angels and archangels
may have gathered there,
Cherubim and seraphim
thronged the air;
But only His mother,
in her maiden bliss,
Worshipped the Beloved
with a kiss.

What can I give Him,
Poor as I am?
If I were a shepherd,
I would bring a lamb,
If I were a Wise Man,
I would do my part,—
Yet what I can I give Him,
Give my heart.[119]

Christina Rossetti (1830–1894), English poet.
Often voted the best and favorite carol.

119. Marsh, *Rossetti*, p. 10.

Go Tell It on the Mountain

Go tell it on the mountain,
Over the hills and everywhere;
Go, tell it on the mountain
That Jesus Christ is born![120]

African-American spiritual, attributed to John Wesley Work II
(1871–1925).

---

120. Keyte, *Carols*, p. 268.

Carol

Three kings from out the Orient
For Judah's land were fairly bent,
To find the Lord of grace;
And as they journeyed pleasantlie,
A star kept shining in the sky,
To guide them to the place.
"O Star," they cried, "by all confest
Withouten dreed, the loveliest!"

The first was Melchior to see
The emperour hight of Arabye,
An aged man, I trow:
He sat upon a rouncy bold,
Had taken of the red red gold,
The babe for to endow.

The next was Caspar, young and gay,
That held the realm of far Cathay—
Our Jesus drew him thence—
Yclad in silk from head to heel,
He rode upon a high cameel,
And bare the frankincense.

The last was dusky Balthasar,
That rode upon a dromedary—
His coat was of the fur.
Dark-browed he came from Samarkand,
The Christ to seek, and in his hand
Upheld the bleeding myrrh.[121]

121. Brooks-Davies, *Christmas Please!*, p. 12.

Thomas Edward Brown (1830–1897), English schoolmaster and "Manx national poet".
Written in an antique style.

I Wonder as I Wander

I wonder as I wander, out under the sky,
How Jesus the Saviour did come for to die
For poor on'ry people like you and like I;
I wonder as I wander out under the sky.

When Mary birthed Jesus, 'twas in a cow's stall,
With wise men and farmers and shepherds and all;
But high from the heavens a star's light did fall,
And the promise of ages it then did recall.

If Jesus had wanted for any wee thing,
A star in the sky or a bird on the wing,
Or all of God's angels in heaven for to sing,
He surely could have had it 'cause he was the King.[122]

John Jacob Niles (1892–1980), based on fragments of a traditional Appalachian song.

122. Keyte, *Carols*, p. 271.

Softly the Night is Sleeping

Softly the night is sleeping on Bethlehem's peaceful hill,
Silent the shepherds watching their gentle flocks are still.
But hark the wondrous music falls from the opening sky,
Valley and cliff re-echo glory to God on high.
Glory to God it rings again,
Peace on the earth, goodwill to men.

Come with the gladsome shepherds quick hastening from the fold,
Come with the wise men bringing incense and myrrh and gold,
Come to Him poor and lowly, all round the cradle throng,
Come with our hearts of sunshine and sing the angels' song.
Glory to God tell out again,
Peace on the earth, goodwill to men.

Wave ye the wreath unfading, the fir tree and the pine,
Green from the snows of winter to deck the holy shrine;
Bring ye the happy children for this is Christmas morn,
Jesus the sinless infant, Jesus the Lord is born.
Glory to God, to God again,
Peace on the earth, goodwill to men.[123]

Sussex, England, traditional.

123. Brooks-Davies, *Christmas Please!*, p. 100.

Favorite Christmas Numbers

"White Christmas": Bing Crosby, 1942.

"Have Yourself a Merry Little Christmas": Judy Garland, 1944.

"The Christmas Song": Nat King Cole, 1945.

"It's Beginning To Look A Lot Like Christmas": Perry Como, 1951.

"It's the Most Wonderful Time of the Year": Andy Williams, 1963.

"I Wish It Could Be Christmas Every Day": Roy Wood, 1973.

"Merry Xmas Everybody": Slade, 1980.

"Do They Know It's Christmas?": Band Aid, 1984.

"Driving Home For Christmas": Chris Rea, 1986.

"Fairytale of New York": The Pogues, 1988.

"All I Want For Christmas is You": Mariah Carey, 1994.

Happy Christmas?

Some downbeat numbers.

"The Little Boy that Santa Claus Forgot": Nat King Cole, 1953.

"Blue Christmas": Elvis Presley, 1957.

"Christmas Without Daddy": Loretta Lynn, 1966.

"Christmas Eve Can Kill You": The Everly Brothers, 1971.

"Please, Daddy, Don't Get Drunk This Christmas": John Denver, 1973.

"Christmas Card From a Hooker in Minneapolis": Tom Waits, 1978.

"Another Lonely Christmas": Prince, 1984.

"Christmas in Prison": John Prine, 1994.

"Christmas Ain't Like Christmas Anymore": Kitty Wells, 2005.

Christmas Past

The First Crib[124]

It happened, three years prior to his death, that [Francis] decided to celebrate at the town of Greccio the memory of the birth of the Child Jesus with the greatest possible solemnity, in order to arouse devotion. So that this would not be considered a type of novelty, he petitioned for and obtained permission from the Supreme Pontiff. He had a manger prepared, hay carried in and an ox and an ass led to the spot. The brethren are summoned, the people arrive, the forest amplifies with their cries, and that venerable night is rendered brilliant and solemn by a multitude of bright lights and by resonant and harmonious hymns of praise. The man of God stands before the manger, filled with piety, bathed in tears, and overcome with joy. A solemn Mass is celebrated over the manger, with Francis, a Levite of Christ, chanting the holy Gospel. Then he preaches to the people standing around him about the birth of the poor King, whom, whenever he means to call him, he called in his tender love, the Babe from Bethlehem. A certain virtuous and truthful knight, Sir John of Greccio . . . claimed that he saw a beautiful little child asleep in that manger whom the blessed father Francis embraced in both of his arms and seemed to wake it from sleep.[125]

St. Bonaventure: *Legends*, 10, 7.

124. The relics of the purported original crib were taken from Bethlehem to Rome in the time of Pope Theodore (642–649) and housed in the church of Sancta Maria ad Praesepe, now Santa Maria Maggiore.

125. Armstrong, *Francis*, 610–611.

Church Ales

In certain townes, where dronken Bacchus beares swaie . . . the
churchwardens of every parishe, with the consent of the whole
parishe, provide halfe a score or twentie quarters of maulte, where-
of some they buy of the church stocke, and some is given to them
of the parishioners themselves, every one conferring somewhat,
according to his abilitie; which maulte being made into very strong
ale or bere, is sette to sale, either in the church or some other place
assigned to that purpose. Then when this is set abroche, well is he
that can gete the soonest to it, and spend the most at it.[126]

Philip Stubbes, *Anatomie of Abuses* (1583).
In Tudor England, church-wardens organized Church Ales to raise
money for the church.

126. Hadfield, *Twelve Days*, p. 52.

Feasting with King James I

The first Christmas of worthy king James was at his court at Hampton, Ao. 1603: wher the French, Spanish & Polonian[127] Ambassadors were severallie solemplie feasted: name plaies & daunces with swordes: one mask[128] by English and Scottish lords: another by the Queen's Maiestie & eleven more ladies of her chamber presenting giftes as goddesses. The maskes, especialli the laste, costes 2000I.[129] or 3000I. the apparells: rare musick, fine songes: & in jewels most riche 20000I., the lest to my iudgment: & her maiestie I0000I. after Christmas was running at Ring[130] by the King & 8 or 9 lords for the honour of those goddesses & then they all feasted together privatelie.[131]

From the Journal of Sir Roger Wilbraham (1553–1616), 1603, an English lawyer.

127. Polish.
128. masque.
129. pounds.
130. equestrian tournament.
131. Hadfield, *Twelve Days*, p. 94.

The Pilgrims' First Christmas

On the day called Christmas-day, the Governor called them out to work (as was used), but the most of this new company excused themselves, and said it went against their consciences to work on that day. So the Governor told them that if they made it a matter of conscience, he would spare them till they were better informed. So he led away the rest, and left them. But they came home at noon from their work, he found them in the street at play openly; some pitching the bar, and some at stool ball, and such like sports. So he went to them, and took away their implements, and told them that was against his conscience that they should play and others work. If they made the keeping of it a matter of devotion, let them keep their houses, but there should be no gaming or reveling in the streets. Since which time nothing hath been attempted that way, at least, openly.[132]

Massachusetts, 1621.
William Bradford, *History of Plymouth Plantation*, 1651.

132. Bella, *Christmas Imperative*, p. 65.

The Terrible Remonstrance

. . . Parliament spent some Time in Consultation about the Abolition of *Christmas*-day, pass'd Orders to that Effect, and resolv'd to sit on the following Day, which was commonly called *Christmas*-day.[133]

The *Flying Eagle Gazette*, London, 24 December 1652, during the English Commonwealth.

133. Lewis, *Christmas*, p. 11.

Arrested on Christmas Day

25 December 1657

I went with my Wife and others to London to celebrate Christmas day. Mr. Gunning preaching in Excester[134] Chapell, on Micah 7:2. Sermon Ended, as he was giving us the holy Sacrament, The Chapell was surrounded with Souldiers. All the Communicants and Assembly surprized and kept Prisoners by them, some in the house, others carried away. It fell to my share to be confined to a roome in the house, where yet were permitted to Dine with the master of it, the Countesse of Dorset, Lady Hatton and some others of quality who invited me. In the afternoone came Collonel Whaly,[135] Goffe, and others from Whitehall to examine us one by one, and some they committed to the Martial, some to Prison, some Committed. When I came before them they tooke my name and aboad, examind me, why contrarie to an Ordinance made that none should any longer observe the superstitious time of the Nativity (so esteem'd by them), I durst offend, and particularly be at Common prayers, which they told me was but the Masse in English, and particularly pray for Charles stuard,[136] for which we had no Scripture. I told them we did not pray for Charles Steward, but for all Christian Kings, Princes, and Governors. The[y] replied, in so doing we praied for the King of Spain too, who was their Enemie, and a Papist, with other frivolous and insnaring questions, with much threatning and finding no colour to detaine me longer, with much pitty of my Ignorance, they dismissed me. These were men of high flight, and above Ordinances, and spake spitefull things of our Blessed Lord's nativity. So I got home late the next day, blessed be God. These wretched miscreants, held their muskets against us as we came up to receive the Sacred Elements as if they would

134. Exeter.
135. Whalley.
136. Charles Stuart, King Charles II.

have shot us at the Altar; but yet suffering us to finish the Office of Communion, as perhaps not in their Instructions what they should do in case they found us in that Action.[137]

John Evelyn (1620–1706), English diarist.
This incident occurred after the execution of King Charles I, during the Protectorate of Oliver Cromwell.

137. Evelyn, *Diary*, p. 383.

The Trial of Old Father Christmas

In 1660, when Christmas was restored along with the English monarchy, some remained opposed to its celebration. *The Examination and Tryal of Old Father Christmas* (1678) pictures Christmas as an old man, tried for encouraging gluttony, drunkenness, and lasciviousness. Here is his defense:

Christmas: My Lord, let the Records be searched, & you shall find, that the Angels rejoiced at my coming, & sung *Gloria in Excelsis*; the Patriarchs and Prophets longed to see me.

The Fathers have sweetly embraced our modern Divines all comfortably cherished me, O let me be not despised now I'm old. Is there not an injunction in *Magna Charta* that commands men to inquire for the old way, which is the good way; many good deeds do I do, O why do the people hate me? We are commanded to be given to Hospitality, & this hath been my practice from my youth upward: I come to put men to mind of their redemption, to have them love one another, to impact with something here below, that they may receive more and better things above . . .[138]

138. Bella, *Christmas Imperative*, p. 62.

"Old Christmas" riding a goat, illustration by Robert Seymour, 1836.

A Christmas Wedding

To church in the morning, and there saw a wedding in the church, which I have not seen many a day; and the young people so merry with one another, and strange, to see what delight we married people have to see these poor fools decoyed into our condition, every man and woman gazing and smiling at them.[139]

Samuel Pepys' *Diary*.
25 December 1665

139. Pepys, *Diary*, p. 564.

At Sea, 1675

Crismas Day we'll keepe thus: At four in the morning our trumpeters all doe flatt their trumpetts, and begin at our Captain's Cabin, and thence to all the officers' and gentlemen's Cabins; playing a levite at each cabin door, and bidding good morrow, wishing a merry Crismas. After they goe to their station, viz. on the poope, and sound three levitts in honour of the morning. At ten we goe to prayers and sermon; text, Zacc. ix, 9. Our Captain had all his officers and gentlemen to dinner with him, where wee had excellent good fayre: a ribb of beefe, plumb-puddings, minct pyes, &c., and plenty of good wines of severall sorts; dranke healths to the King, to our wives and friends, and ended the day with much civil myrth.[140]

Diary of Rev. Henry Teonge (1621–1690), chaplain, H.M.S. *Assistance*.

140. Lewis, *Christmas*, p. 43.

Profane Christ-Mass Keeping

The generality of Christmas-keepers observe that Festival after such a manner as is highly dishonourable to the name of Christ. How few are there comparatively that spend those Holidays (as they are called) after an Holy manner. But they are consumed in Compotations, in Interludes, in playing at Cards, in Revellings, in excess of Wine, in mad Mirth; Will Christ the holy Son of God be pleased with such services? Just after this manner were the Saturnalia of the Heathen celebrated. Saturn was the gaming god . . . [T]he Feast of Christ's Nativity is attended with such Profaneness, as that it deserves the name of Saturns Mass, or of Bacchus his Mass, or if you will, the Devils Mass, rather than to have the Holy name of Christ put upon it. Mr. Perkins[141] justly complains that, The Feast of Christ's Nativity (commonly so called) is not spent in praising God, but in Revelling, Dicing, Carding, Masking, Mumming, and in all Licentious Liberty for the most part, as though it were some Heathen Feast of Ceres or Bacchus. And Latimer[142] in one of his Sermons saith, That men dishonour Christ more in the 12 Days of Christmas, than in all the 12 Months besides.[143]

from Increase Mather, *A Testimony Against several Prophane Customs,* London, 1687.

141. William Perkins, English Puritan (1558–1602).
142. Hugh Latimer, Bishop of Worcester (1487–1555).
143. Mather, *Testimony,* p. 44.

A Frenchman's English Christmas

From Christmas Day till after Twelfth Day is a time of Christian rejoicing; a mixture of devotion and pleasure: They wish one another happiness; they give treats, and make it their whole business to drive away melancholy... In the taverns the landlord gives part of what is eaten and drank in his house that and the two next days; for instance they reckon you for the wine, and tell you there is nothing to pay for bread, nor your slice of Westphalia [ham]. Every family against Christmas makes a famous pie, which they call Christmas pie: it is a great nostrum the composition of this pasty; It is a most learned mixture of neats-tongues, chicken, eggs, sugar, raisins, lemon, and orange peel, various kinds of spicery, etc. They also make a sort of soup with plums, which is not at all inferior to the pie, which is in their language called plum-porridge.[144]

Henri Misson de Valbourg (fl. 1698), French poet.

144. Misson, *Memoirs*, p. 34

George Washington's Present List

for his young stepson and stepdaughter, Christmas 1759.

Bird on bellows
Cuckoo
Turnabout parrot
Grocer's shop
Aviary
Prussian dragoon
Man smoking
Tunbridge tea-set
Three neat books
Tea-chest
Straw parchment box with a glass
Neat dressed wax baby[145]

145. Moran, *Christmases*, p. 5.

Christmas Dinner, at New College, Oxford

25 December 1773

We had a very handsome Dinner of my ordering as I order Dinner every Day being Sub-Warden.

We had for dinner two fine Codds boiled with Fryed Soals round them & Oyster Sauce, a fine Surloin of Beef roasted, Some Peas Soup & an Orange Pudding for the first Cours, for the Second we had a Lease of Wild Ducks rosted, a fore-Qr: of Lamb & sallad & Mince Pies—We had a Grace Cup before the second Course brought by the Butler to the Steward of the Hall who was Mr. Adams a Senior Fellow, who got out of his Place & came to my Chair and there drank to me out of it, wishing me a merry Xmas. I then took it of him & drank wishing him the same & then it went round, three standing up all the time. From the high Table the Grace Cup goes to the Batchelors & Scholars. After the second Course there was a fine Plumb Cake brought to the Senr. Table as is usual on this Day, which also goes to the Batchelors after—After Grace is said there is another Grace-Cup to drink *omnibus Wiccamisis*,[146] which is drunk as the first, only the Steward of the Hall does not attend the second Grace Cup . . .

N.B. Put on this Day a new Coat and Waistcoat for the first Time.[147]

James Woodforde (1740–1803), *The Diary of a Country Parson 1758–1802.*

146. 'for all Wykehamists'; New College was founded by William of Wykeham in 1379.
147. Winstanley, *Diary*, p. 195.

Christmas at Christ's Hospital, London

Let me have leave to remember the festivities at Christmas, when the richest of us would club our stock to have a gaudy day, sitting round the fire, replenished to the height with logs; and the penny-less and he that could contribute nothing, partook in all the mirth and in some of the substantialities of the feasting; the carol sung by night at that time of the year, which, when a young boy, I have so often lain awake to hear from seven (the hour of going to bed) till ten, when it was sung by the older boys and monitors, and have listened to it, in their rude chanting, till I have been transported in fancy to the fields of Bethlehem, and the song of which was sung at that season by the angels' voices to the shepherds.[148]

Charles Lamb (1775–1834), English author, best known for his *Tales from Shakespeare*.

148. Smith, *Christmas Reader*, p. 256.

Infant Seraphs

While I lay musing on my pillow, I heard the sound of little feet pattering outside of the door, and a whispering consultation. Presently a choir of small voices chanted forth an old Christmas carol, the burden of which was:

Rejoice, our Savior He was born

On Christmas Day in the morning.

I rose softly, slipped on my clothes, opened the door suddenly, and beheld one of the most beautiful little fairy groups that a painter could imagine. It consisted of a boy and two girls, the eldest not more than six, and lovely as seraphs. They were going the rounds of the house, and singing at every chamber door; but my sudden appearance frightened them into mute bashfulness. They remained for a moment playing on their lips with their fingers, and now and then stealing a shy glance from under their eyebrows, until, as if by one impulse, they scampered away, and as they turned an angle of the gallery I heard them laughing in triumph at their escape.[149]

From the American author Washington Irving (1783–1859), "Old Christmas and Bracebridge Hall", in *The Sketch Book of Geoffrey Crayon, Gent.*, 1818–19, a largely fictional account.

149. *Northern Advertiser*, p. 4.

Quakers Against Christmas

That particular period of time, especially, called Christmas, viewed as a Religious festival, has, we fully believe tended more to open licentiousness of manners, than to the increase and encouragement of sound morality and religion. The mummery which takes place in some of the churches, so called, at this season, under the ministration of a class of hireling teachers, and the childish and superficial ideas which are propagated through this corrupt and interested medium, concerning the nature and mode of Christian redemption, are wonderfully calculated to enlarge the sphere of stupidity, and to increase the shades of moral darkness over the minds of mankind.[150]

"The Season", in *Friends' Intelligencer*, Philadelphia, January 3 1846.

150. Shoemaker, *Pennsylvania*, p. xviii.

Dickens' Christmas List

I have been looking on, this evening, at a merry company of children assembled round that pretty German toy, a Christmas Tree.... It was brilliantly lighted by a multitude of little tapers; and everywhere sparkled and glittered with bright objects. There were rosy-cheeked dolls, hiding behind the green leaves; and there were real watches (with movable hands, at least, and an endless capacity of being wound up) dangling from innumerable twigs; there were French-polished tables, chairs, bedsteads, wardrobes, eight-day clocks, and various other articles of domestic furniture (wonderfully made, in tin, at Wolverhampton); perched among the boughs, as if in preparation for some fairy-house-keeping; there were jolly, broad-faced little men, much more agreeable in appearance than many real men—and no wonder, for their heads took off, and showed them to be full of sugar-plums; there were fiddles and drums; there were tambourines, books, work-boxes, paint-boxes, sweetmeat-boxes, peep-show boxes, and all kinds of boxes; there were trinkets for the elder girls, far brighter than any grown-up gold and jewels; there were baskets and pin-cushions in all devices; there were guns, swords, and banners; there were witches standing in enchanted rings of pasteboard, to tell fortunes; there were teetotums, humming-tops, needle-cases, pen-wipers, smelling-bottles, conversation-cards, bouquet-holders; real fruit, made artificially dazzling with gold leaf; imitation apples, pears, and walnuts, crammed with surprises; in short, as a pretty child, before me, delightedly whispered to another pretty child, her bosom friend, "There was everything, and more."[151]

from Charles Dickens, *A Christmas Tree*, 1850.

151. Dickens, *Christmas Tree*, p. 127.

"Putting up the Christmas", illustration by Frederick Walker, 1860.

At the Court of Queen Victoria

The tree employed for this festive purpose is a young fir of about eight feet high, and has six tiers of branches. On each tier, or branch, are arranged a dozen wax tapers. Pendant from the branches are elegant trays, baskets, bonbonnières, and other receptacles for sweetmeats of the most varied and expensive kind; and of all forms, colours and degrees of beauty. Fancy cakes, gilt gingerbread and eggs filled with sweetmeats, are also suspended by variously-coloured ribbons from the branches. The tree, which stands upon a table covered with white damask, is supported at the root by piles of sweets of a larger kind, and by toys and dolls of all descriptions, suited to the youthful fancy, and to the several ages of the interesting scions of Royalty for whose gratification they are displayed.[152]

From *The Illustrated London News*, 1848.
Victoria's husband, Prince Albert, introduced the Christmas tree from his native Germany.

152. Hadfield, *Twelve Days*, p. 35.

The Accursed Thing

On Christmas Day of this year 1857 our villa saw a very unusual sight. My father had given strictest charge that no difference whatever was to be made in our meals on that day: the dinner was to be neither more copious than usual nor less so. He was obeyed, but the servants, secretly rebellious, made a small plum-pudding for themselves . . . Early in the afternoon, the maids . . . kindly remarked that "the poor dear child ought to have a bit, anyhow", and wheedled me into the kitchen, where I ate a slice of plum-pudding. Shortly I began to feel that pain inside which in my frail state was inevitable, and my conscience smote me violently. At length I could bear my spiritual anguish no longer, and bursting into the study I called out: "Oh! Papa, Papa, I have eaten of flesh offered to idols!" It took some time, between my sobs, to explain what had happened. Then my father sternly said: "Where is the accursed thing?" I explained that as much as was left of it was still on the kitchen table. He took me by the hand, and ran with me into the midst of the startled servants, seized what remained of the pudding, and with the plate in one hand and me still tight in the other, ran till we reached the dust-heap, when he flung the idolatrous confectionery on to the middle of the ashes, and then raked it deep down into the mass. The suddenness, the violence, the velocity of this extraordinary act made an impression on my memory which nothing will ever efface.[153]

Edmund Gosse (1849–1928). Gosse's father, Philip, was a strict adherent of the Plymouth Brethren sect.

153. Gosse, *Father*, p. 111.

No Presents

"Christmas won't be Christmas without any presents," grumbled Jo, lying on the rug.

"It's so dreadful to be poor!" sighed Meg, looking down at her old dress.

"I don't think it's fair for some girls to have plenty of pretty things, and other girls nothing at all," added little Amy, with an injured sniff . . . .

Nobody spoke for a minute; then Meg said in an altered tone, "You know the reason Mother proposed not having any presents this Christmas was because it is going to be a hard winter for everyone; and she thinks we ought not to spend money for pleasure, when our men are suffering so in the army. We can't do much, but we can make our little sacrifices, and ought to do it gladly. But I am afraid I don't." And Meg shook her head, as she thought regretfully of all the pretty things she wanted.

"But I don't think the little we should spend would do any good. We've each got a dollar, and the army wouldn't be much helped by our giving that. I agree not to expect anything from mother or you, but I do want to buy *Undine and Sintram* for myself. I've wanted it *so* long," said Jo, who was a bookworm.

"I planned to spend mine on new music," said Beth, with a little sigh, which no one heard but the hearth-brush and kettle-holder.

"I shall get a nice box of Faber's drawing pencils. I really need them," said Amy decidedly.[154]

Louisa M. Alcott (1832–1888), American author.

154. Alcott, *Little Women*, p. 3.

Household Duties

In December, the principal household duty lies in preparing for the creature comforts of those near and dear to us, so as to meet old Christmas with a happy face, a contented mind, and a full larder; and in stoning the plums, washing the currants, cutting the citron, beating the eggs, and MIXING THE PUDDING, a housewife is not unworthily greeting the genial season of all good things.[155]

Mrs. Beeton (1836–1865), English editor, the Martha Stewart of her day.

---

155. Beeton, *Household*, p. 38.

A Frosty Christmas

As I lay awake praying in the early morning I thought I heard a sound of distant bells. It was an intense frost. I sat down in my bath upon a sheet of thick ice which broke in the middle into large pieces whilst sharp points and jagged edges stuck all round the sides of the tub like *chevaux de frise*,[156] not particularly comforting to the naked thighs and loins, for the keen ice cut like broken glass. The ice water stung and scorched like fire. I had to collect the floating pieces of ice and pile them on a chair before I could use the sponge and then I had to thaw the sponge in my hands for it was a mass of ice. The morning was most brilliant. Walked to the Sunday School with Gibbins and the road sparkled with millions of rainbows, the seven colours gleaming in every glittering point of hoar frost. The Church was very cold in spite of two roaring stove fires. Mr. V.[157] preached and went to Bettws.[158]

Christmas Day 1870.
From the diary of the Revd. Francis Kilvert (1840–1879), curate at Clyro, on the Welsh border.

156. Row of spikes or broken glass placed as an obstacle on top of a wall.
157. Richard Lister Venables, vicar of Clyro.
158. Village in South Wales. Plomer, *Kilvert*, p. 127.

Christmas Preparations

Writing Christmas letters all the morning. In the afternoon I went to the Church with Dora and Teddy to put up Christmas decorations. Dora has been very busy for some days past making the straw letters for the Christmas text. Fair Rosamund and good Elizabeth Knight came to the Church to help us and worked heartily and well. They had made some pretty ivy knots and bunches for the pulpit panels and the ivy blossoms cleverly whitened with flour looked just like white flowers.

The churchwarden Jacob Knight was sitting by his sister in front of the roaring fire. We were talking of the death of Major Torrens on the ice at Corsham pond yesterday. Speaking of people slipping and falling on ice the good churchwarden sagely remarked, "Some do fall on their faces and some do fall on their rumps. And they as do hold their selves uncommon stiff do most in generally fall on their rumps."

I took old John Bryant a Christmas packet of tea and sugar and raisins from my Mother. The old man had covered himself almost entirely over in his bed to keep himself warm, like a marmot in its nest. He said, "If I live till New Year's Day I shall have seen ninety-six New Years." He said also, "I do often see things flying about me, thousands and thousands of them about half the size of a large pea, and they are red, white, blue, and yellow, and all colours. I asked Mr. Morgan what they were and he said they were the spirits of just men made perfect."[159]

Francis Kilvert, Christmas Eve 1874.
He was currently serving as curate to his father at Langley Burrell, Wiltshire, England.

159. Plomer, *Kilvert*, p. 372.

Kneeling Cattle

Speaking of the . . . kneeling and weeping of the oxen in old Christmas Eve (to-night) Priscilla said, "I have known old James Meredith 40 years and I have never known him far from the truth, and I said to him one day, 'James, tell me the truth, did you ever see the oxen kneel on old Christmas Eve at the Weston?' And he said, 'No, I never saw them kneel at the Weston but when I was at Hinton at Staunton-on-Wye I saw them. I was watching them on old Christmas Eve and at 12 o'clock the oxen that were standing knelt down upon their knees and those that were lying down rose up on their knees and there they stayed kneeling and moaning, the tears running down their faces.'"[160]

Francis Kilvert's diary, 4 January, 1878. Some English farmers believed that cattle and oxen knelt in adoration at midnight on 5 January, Christmas Eve in the old calendar.

160. Plomer, *Kilvert*, p. 442.

The Oxen

Christmas Eve, and twelve of the clock,
"Now they are all on their knees,"
An elder said as we sat in a flock
By the embers in hearthside ease.

We pictured the meek mild creatures where
They dwelt in their strawy pen,
Nor did it occur to one of us there
To doubt they were kneeling then.

So fair a fancy few would weave
In these years! Yet, I feel,
If someone said on Christmas Eve,
"Come, see the oxen kneel

In the lonely barton by yonder coomb
Our childhood used to know,"
I should go with him in the gloom,
Hoping it might be so.[161]

Thomas Hardy (1840–1928), English poet and novelist.
Hardy's poem reflects the belief recorded by Kilvert above.

161. Batchelor, *Christian Poetry*, p. 264.

Anger in the West Gallery

The music on Christmas mornings was frequently below the standard of church-performances at other times. The boys were sleepy from the heavy exertions of the night; the men were slightly wearied; and now, in addition to these constant reasons, there was a dampness in the atmosphere that still further aggravated the evil. Their strings, from the recent long exposure to the night air, rose whole semitones, and snapped with a loud twang at the most silent moment; which necessitated more retiring than ever to the back of the gallery, and made the gallery throats quite husky with the quantity of coughing and hemming required for tuning in. The vicar looked cross.

When the singing was in progress there was suddenly discovered to be a strong and shrill reinforcement from some point, ultimately found to be the school-girls' aisle. At every attempt it grew bolder and more distinct. At the third time of singing, these intrusive feminine voices were as mighty as those of the regular singers; in fact, the flood of sound from this quarter assumed such an individuality, that it had a time, a key, almost a tune of its own, surging upwards when the gallery plunged downwards, and the reverse.

Now this had never happened before within the memory of man. The girls, like the rest of the congregation had always been humble and respectful followers of the gallery; singing at sixes and sevens if without gallery leaders; never interfering with the ordinances of these practised artists—having no will, union, power, or proclivity except it was given them from the established choir enthroned above them.

A good deal of desperation became noticeable in the gallery throats and strings, which continued throughout the musical portion of the service. Directly the fiddles were laid down, Mr. Penny's spectacles put in their sheath, and the text had been given out, an indignant whispering began.

"Did ye hear that, souls?" Mr. Penny said, in a groaning breath.

"Brazen-faced hussies!" said Bowman.

"True; why, they were every note as loud as we, fiddles and all, if not louder!"

"Fiddles and all!" echoed Bowman bitterly.

"Shall anything bolder be found than united 'ooman?" Mr. Spinks murmured.

"What I want to know is," said the tranter (as if he knew already, but that civilization required the form of words), "what business people have to tell maidens to sing like that when they don't sit in a gallery, and never have entered one in their lives? That's the question, my sonnies."

"'Tis the gallery have got to sing, all the world knows," said Mr. Penny. "Why, souls, what's the use o' the ancients spending scores of pounds to build galleries if people down in the lowest depths of the church sing like that at a moment's notice?"[162]

From Thomas Hardy, *Under the Greenwood Tree*, 1872.

---

162. Hardy, *Greenwood*, p. 41.

Absent Friends

The annual invitation came to spend Christmas with Carrie's mother—the usual family festive gathering to which we always look forward. Lupin[163] declined to go. I was astounded, and expressed my surprise and disgust. Lupin then obliged us with the following radical speech: "I hate a family gathering at Christmas. What does it mean? Why, someone says: 'Ah! we miss poor Uncle James, who was here last year,' and we all begin to snivel. Someone else says: 'It's two years since poor Aunt Liz used to sit in that corner.' Then we all begin to snivel again. Then another gloomy relation says: 'Ah! I wonder whose turn it will be next?' Then we all snivel again, and proceed to eat and drink too much; and they don't discover until *I* get up that we have been seated thirteen at dinner."[164]

From George and Weedon Grossmith, *The Diary of a Nobody*, 1892.

163. Son of the fictional diarist, Mr. Pooter.
164. Grossmith, *Diary*, p. 104.

An Atrocious Institution

Like all intelligent people, I greatly dislike Christmas. It revolts me to see a whole nation refrain from music for weeks together in order that every man may rifle his neighbour's pockets under cover of a ghastly general pretence of festivity. It is really an atrocious institution, this Christmas.

We must be gluttonous because it is Christmas. We must be drunken because it is Christmas. We must be insincerely generous; we must buy things that nobody wants, and give them to people we don't like; we must go to absurd entertainments, that make even our little children satirical; we must writhe under venal officiousness from legions of freebooters, all because it is Christmas—that is, because the mass of the population, including the all powerful middle class tradesmen, depend on a week of licence and brigandage, waste and intemperance, to clear off its outstanding liabilities at the end of the year. As for me, I shall fly from it all tomorrow or next day to some remote spot miles from a shop, where nothing worse can befall me than a serenade from a few peasants, or some equally harmless survival of medieval mummery, shyly proffered, not advertised, moderate in its expectations, and soon over.[165]

George Bernard Shaw (1856–1950), Irish playwright, author of *Pygmalion.*

165. Shaw, *Music*, p. 113.

Lady Bountiful

A lady had made a present of a Christmas-tree to the children of a workhouse, and she invited me to go with her and assist at the distribution of the toys. There was a drive through the early dusk of a very cold Christmas eve, followed by the drawing up of a lamp-lit brougham in the snowy quadrangle of a grim-looking charitable institution. I had never been in an English workhouse before, and this one transported me, with the aid of memory, to the early pages of "Oliver Twist". We passed through cold, bleak passages, to which an odour of suet-pudding, the aroma of Christmas cheer, failed to impart an air of hospitality; and then, after waiting a while in a little parlour appertaining to the superintendent, where the remainder of a dinner of by no means eleemosynary simplicity and the attitude of a gentleman asleep with a flushed face on the sofa seemed to effect a tacit exchange of references, we were ushered into a large frigid refectory, chiefly illumined by the twinkling tapers of the Christmas-tree. Here entered to us some hundred and fifty little children of charity, who had been making a copious dinner and who brought with them an atmosphere of hunger memorably satisfied—together with other traces of the occasion upon their pinafores and their small red faces . . . They filed up and received their little offerings, and then they compressed themselves into a tight infantine bunch and, lifting up their small hoarse voices, directed a melancholy hymn toward their benefactress. The scene was a picture I shall not forget, with its curious mixture of poetry and sordid prose—the dying wintry light in the big bare, stale room; the beautiful Lady Bountiful, standing in the twinkling glory of the Christmas-tree; the little multitude of staring and wondering, yet perfectly expressionless, faces.[166]

Henry James (1843–1916), American-British author, 1905.

166. James, *English Hours*, pp. 154–155.

In the Midst of War

This is a strange Christmas Eve. Almost the whole world is locked in deadly struggle. Armed with the most terrible weapons which science can devise, the nations advance upon each other . . . .

Here, in the midst of war, raging and roaring over all the lands and seas, creeping nearer to our hearts and homes; here, amid all these tumults, we have tonight the peace of the spirit in each cottage home and in every generous heart.

Therefore, we might cast aside—for this night at least—the cares and dangers which beset us, and make for the children an evening of happiness in a world of storm. Here then—for one night only—each home throughout the English-speaking world should be a brightly lighted island of happiness and peace.

Let the children have their night of fun and laughter. Let the gifts of Father Christmas delight their play. Let us grownups share to the full in their unstinted pleasures, before we turn again to the stern task and the formidable year that lie before us.

Resolve that by our sacrifice and daring, these same children shall not be robbed of their inheritance, or denied their right to live in a free and decent world.

And so, in God's Mercy, a Happy Christmas to you all.[167]

Winston Churchill, a speech broadcast to the world from the White House, Washington D.C., 24 December 1941.

---

167. Roosevelt Library, 197366.

Carol-singing

The week before Christmas, when snow seemed to lie thickest, was the moment for carol-singing; and when I think back to those nights it is to the crunch of snow and to the lights of the lanterns on it.. . . .

Steadily we worked through the length of the valley, going from house to house, visiting the lesser and the greater gentry—the farmers, the doctors, the merchants, the majors, and other exalted persons. It was freezing hard and blowing too; yet not for a moment did we feel the cold. The snow blew into our faces, into our eyes and mouths, soaked through our puttees, got into our boots, and dripped from our woollen caps. But we did not care . . .

We approached our last house high up on the hill, the place of Joseph the farmer. For him we had chosen a special carol, which was about the other Joseph, so that we always felt that singing it added a spicy cheek to the night . . .

We grouped ourselves round the farmhouse porch. The sky cleared, and broad streams of stars ran down over the valley and away to Wales . . . Everything was quiet; everywhere there was the faint crackling silence of the winter night. We started singing, and we were all moved by the words and the sudden trueness of our voices. Pure, very clear, and breathless we sang . . .[168]

From *Cider With Rosie,* by Laurie Lee (1914–1997).

168. Lee, *Rosie*, pp. 172, 176–178.

Best-selling Xmas

Rudolph the Red-Nosed Reindeer was almost named Reginald, or Rollo. Illinois-based copywriter Robert L. May (1905–1976) introduced Rudolph in coloring-books designed for the department store Montgomery Ward in 1939. Rudolph's nose wasn't supposed to be red since the publisher didn't want him linked with alcohol.

Singer Brenda Lee (1944–), "Little Miss Dynamite", recorded the original version of "Rockin' Around the Christmas Tree" while aged only thirteen.

Around half the top 25 best-selling Christmas numbers are by Jewish composers, including "Let It Snow!", "The Christmas Song", "Silver Bells", "Baby, It's Cold Outside", "White Christmas", "Rudolph the Red-Nosed Reindeer", "Winter Wonderland", and "I'll Be Home for Christmas".

Bing Crosby's "White Christmas" is not only the best-selling Christmas song but the all-time best-selling single.

Church leaders in Boston tried to ban "I Saw Mommy Kissing Santa Claus", recorded in 1952 by Jimmy Boyd, aged thirteen. However, in the first week the disc sold 2 million copies.

Christmas lights

1882: First working electric lights on a Christmas tree—at the Manhattan home of Edward H. Johnson, friend of Thomas Edison.

1901: General Electric (GE) first marketed individual electric lights for Christmas trees.

1903: Ever-Ready introduced sets of eight lights, wired together in a string.

1909: GE first marketed Christmas light-bulbs shaped like Santa and snowmen.

1920s: Cone- and flame-shaped bulbs introduced.

1927: GE introduced parallel wiring, so lights in a series remained lit after one burned out.

1930s: First appearance of bubble lights.

The Nativity in Scripture

The Annunciation

Now the birth of Jesus Christ was on this wise: When as his mother Mary was espoused to Joseph, before they came together, she was found with child of the Holy Ghost. Then Joseph her husband, being a just man, and not willing to make her a publick example, was minded to put her away privily. But while he thought on these things, behold, the angel of the Lord appeared unto him in a dream, saying, Joseph, thou son of David, fear not to take unto thee Mary thy wife: for that which is conceived in her is of the Holy Ghost. And she shall bring forth a son, and thou shalt call his name JESUS: for he shall save his people from their sins.

Matthew 1:18–21, King James Version, 1611.

The Magnificat

My soul doth magnify the Lord: and my spirit hath rejoiced in God
  my Savior.
For he hath regarded: the lowliness of his handmaiden:
For, behold, from henceforth: all generations shall call me blessed.
For he that is mighty hath magnified me: and holy is his name.
And his mercy is on them that fear him: throughout all generations.
He hath showed strength with his arm: he hath scattered the proud
  in the imagination of their hearts.
He hath put down the mighty from their seat: and hath exalted the
  humble and meek.
He hath filled the hungry with good things: and the rich he hath
  sent empty away.
He remembering his mercy hath holpen his servant Israel: as he
  promised to our forefathers, Abraham and his seed for ever.[169]

Luke 1:46–55.

169. Book of Common Prayer.

Shepherds Abiding

And there were in the same region shepherds abiding in the field and watching their flock by night. And lo: the angel of the Lord stood hard by them, and the brightness of the Lord shone round about them, and they were sore afraid. But the angel said unto them: Be not afraid. For behold, I bring you tidings of great joy that shall come to all the people; for unto you is born this day in the city of David a savior which is Christ the Lord. And take this for a sign: ye shall find the child swaddled and laid in a manger. And straightway there was with the angel a multitude of heavenly soldiers, lauding God and saying: Glory to God on high, and peace on the earth, and unto men rejoicing.[170]

Luke 2:8–14, William Tyndale's New Testament, 1534.

170. Tyndale, *New Testament*, p. 107.

The Visit of the Wise Men

In the time of King Herod, after Jesus was born in Bethlehem of Judea, wise men from the East came to Jerusalem, asking, "Where is the child who has been born king of the Jews? For we observed his star at its rising, and have come to pay him homage." When King Herod heard this, he was frightened, and all Jerusalem with him; and calling together all the chief priests and scribes of the people, he inquired of them where the Messiah was to be born. They told him, "In Bethlehem of Judea; for so it has been written by the prophet:

'And you, Bethlehem, in the land of Judah,
are by no means least among the rulers of Judah;
for from you shall come a ruler
who is to shepherd my people Israel.'"

Then Herod secretly called for the wise men and learned from them the exact time when the star had appeared. Then he sent them to Bethlehem, saying, "Go and search diligently for the child; and when you have found him, bring me word so that I may also go and pay him homage." When they had heard the king, they set out; and there, ahead of them, went the star that they had seen at its rising, until it stopped over the place where the child was. When they saw that the star had stopped, they were overwhelmed with joy. On entering the house, they saw the child with Mary his mother; and they knelt down and paid him homage. Then, opening their treasure-chests, they offered him gifts of gold, frankincense, and myrrh. And having been warned in a dream not to return to Herod, they left for their own country by another road.

Matthew 2:1–12, Nrsv.

Christmas Verse

St. George and the Dragon

Enter FATHER CHRISTMAS
Here come I, old Father Christmas,
Welcome, or welcome not,
I hope old Father Christmas
Will never be forgot.

I am not come here for to laugh or to jeer,
But for a pocketfull of money, and a skinfull of beer;
To show some sport and pastime,
Gentlemen and ladies, in the Christmas time.
If you will not believe what I do say,
Come in the Turkish Knight—clear the way.
Enter the TURKISH KNIGHT[171]

Extract from *The Christmas Play of St. George and the Dragon*, a
Christmas mumming from the West of England.
Anonymous.

171. Sandys, *Christmastide*, p. 208.

A Christmas Legend

Some say that ever 'gainst that season comes
Wherein our Saviour's birth is celebrated,
This bird of dawning singeth all night long;
And then, they say, no spirit dare stir abroad,
The nights are wholesome, then no planets strike,
No fairy takes, nor witch hath power to charm,
So hallow'd and so gracious is that time.[172]

William Shakespeare (1564–1616), English playwright.

172. Shakespeare: *Hamlet*, p. 177.

A New-yeares Gift Sent to Sir Simeon Steward

. . . but here a jolly
Verse crown'd with Yvie and Holly;
That tels of Winters Tales and Mirth,
That Milk-maids make about the hearth,
Of Christmas sports, the Wassell-boule,
That's tost up, after Fox-i'th'hole:
Of Blind-man-buffe, and of the care
That young men have to shooe the Mare:
Of twelf-tide Cakes, of Pease and Beanes
Wherewith ye make those merry Sceanes . . .
And thus, throughout, with Christmas playes,
Frolick the full twelve Holy-dayes.[173]

Robert Herrick (1591–1674), English poet.
Excerpt.

173. Martin, *Herrick*, p. 126.

Advice

Now that the time has come wherein
Our Savior Christ was born,
The larder's full of beef and pork,
The granary's full of corn.
As God hath plenty to thee sent,
Take comfort of thy labors
And let it never thee repent,
To feed thy needy neighbors.[174]

Anonymous.
From *Poor Robin's Almanack*, 1700.

---

174. Heinz, *Christmas*, pp. 134–135.

Little Jack Horner

Little Jack Horner
Sat in the corner
Eating a Christmas pie.
He put in his thumb
And pulled out a plum,
And said, what a good boy am I.[175]

Anonymous.

175. Hadfield, *Twelve Days*, p. 93.

Christmas is Coming

Christmas is coming, the geese are getting fat,
Please to put a penny in the old man's hat;
If you haven't got a penny, a ha'penny will do,
If you haven't got a ha'penny, God bless you.[176]

Anonymous.

176. Brown, *Christmas Facts*, p. 9.

The Night Before Christmas

'Twas the night before Christmas, when all through the house
Not a creature was stirring, not even a mouse;
The stockings were hung by the chimney with care,
In hopes that St. Nicholas soon would be there;

The children were nestled all snug in their beds,
While visions of sugar-plums danced in their heads;
And Mamma in her kerchief, and I in my cap,
Had just settled our brains for a long winter's nap,

When out on the lawn there arose such a clatter,
I sprang from my bed to see what was the matter.
Away to the window I flew like a flash,
Tore open the shutters and threw up the sash.

The moon on the breast of the new-fallen snow,
Gave a lustre of midday to objects below,
When, what to my wondering eyes should appear,
But a miniature sleigh, and eight tiny reindeer,

With a little old driver, so lively and quick,
I knew in a moment it must be St. Nick.
More rapid than eagles his coursers they came,
And he whistled and shouted, and called them by name:

"Now, *Dasher*! now, *Dancer*! now, *Prancer* and *Vixen*!
On, *Comet*! on, *Cupid*! on, *Donder* and *Blitzen*!
To the top of the porch! to the top of the wall!
Now dash away! dash away! dash away, all!"

As dry leaves that before the wild hurricane fly,
When they meet with an obstacle, mount to the sky,
So up to the house-top the coursers they flew,
With the sleigh full of Toys, and St. Nicholas too.

And then, in a twinkling, I heard on the roof
The prancing and pawing of each little hoof.
As I drew in my head, and was turning around,
Down the chimney St. Nicholas came with a bound.

He was dressed all in fur, from his head to his foot,
And his clothes were all tarnished with ashes and soot;
A bundle of Toys he had slung on his back,
And he looked like a pedlar just opening his pack.

His eyes—how they twinkled! his dimples how merry!
His cheeks were like roses, his nose like a cherry!
His droll little mouth was drawn up like a bow,
And the beard on his chin was as white as the snow;

The stump of a pipe he held tight in his teeth,
And the smoke it encircled his head like a wreath;
He had a broad face and a little round belly,
That shook when he laughed, like a bowlful of jelly.

He was chubby and plump, a right jolly old elf,
And I laughed when I saw him, in spite of myself;
A wink of his eye and a twist of his head
Soon gave me to know I had nothing to dread.

He spoke not a word, but went straight to his work,
And filled all the stockings; then turned with a jerk,
And laying his finger aside of his nose,
And giving a nod, up the chimney he rose;

He sprang to his sleigh, to his team gave a whistle,
And away they all flew like the down of a thistle.
But I heard him exclaim, ere he drove out of sight,
Happy Christmas to all, and to all a good night.[177]

Generally attributed to Clement Clarke Moore (1779–1863), but
possibly by Henry Livingston (1748–1828). A much-parodied but
enduringly popular piece.

177. Moore, *Night*, pp. 113–116.

A Christmas Carol

There's a song in the air! There's a star in the sky!
There's a mother's deep prayer and a baby's low cry!
And the star rains its fire
while the Beautiful sing,
For the manger of Bethlehem
cradles a king.[178]

Josiah Gilbert Holland (1819–1881), editor of *Scribner's Magazine*.
Opening stanza.

178. Holland, *Poetical Writings*, p. 476.

The Christmas Goose

Mr. Smiggs was a gentleman,
And lived in London town;
His wife she was a good kind soul,
And seldom known to frown.

'Twas on Christmas eve,
And Smiggs and his wife lay cosy in bed,
When the thought of buying a goose
Came into his head.

So the next morning,
Just as the sun rose,
He jump'd out of bed,
And he donn'd his clothes,

Saying, "Peggy, my dear.
You need not frown,
For I'll buy you the best goose
In all London town."

So away to the poultry shop he goes,
And bought the goose, as he did propose,
And for it he paid one crown,
The finest, he thought, in London town.

When Smiggs bought the goose
He suspected no harm,
But a naughty boy stole it
From under his arm.

Then Smiggs he cried, "Stop, thief!
Come back with my goose!"
But the naughty boy laugh'd at him,
And gave him much abuse.

But a policeman captur'd the naughty boy,
And gave the goose to Smiggs,
And said he was greatly bother'd
By a set of juvenile prigs.[179]

So Smiggs ran home to his dear Peggy,
Saying, "Hurry, and get this fat goose ready,
That I have bought for one crown;
So, my darling, you need not frown."

"Dear Mr. Smiggs, I will not frown:
I'm sure 'tis cheap for one crown,
Especially at Christmas time—
Oh! Mr. Smiggs, it's really fine."

"Peggy, it is Christmas time,
So let us drive dull care away,
For we have got a Christmas goose,
So cook it well, I pray.

"No matter how the poor are clothed,
Or if they starve at home,
We'll drink our wine, and eat our goose,
Aye, and pick it to the bone."[180]

William Topaz McGonagall (1825–1902), self-styled Scots "poet and tragedian", notorious as an exceedingly bad writer.

179. petty thief or pickpocket.
180. McGonagall, *Poems*, p. 66.

Christmas-greetings [from a fairy to a child]

Lady dear, if Fairies may
For a moment lay aside
Cunning tricks and elfish play,
'Tis at happy Christmas-tide.

We have heard the children say—
Gentle children, whom we love—
Long ago, on Christmas Day,
Came a message from above.

Still, as Christmas-tide come round,
They remember it again—
Echo still the joyful sound
"Peace on earth, good-will to men!"

Yet the hearts must childlike be
Where such heavenly guests abide;
Unto children, in their glee,
All the year is Christmas-tide!

Thus, forgetting tricks and play
For a moment, Lady dear,
We would wish you, if we may,
Merry Christmas, glad New Year![181]

Lewis Carroll (Charles Lutwidge Dodgson, 1832–1898), author of
Alice in Wonderland.

181. Carroll, *Works*, p. 15.

Christmas Day in the Workhouse

It is Christmas Day in the Workhouse,
And the cold bare walls are bright
With garlands of green and holly,
And the place is a pleasant sight:
For with clean-washed hands and faces,
In a long and hungry line
The paupers sit at the tables,
For this is the hour they dine.

And the guardians and their ladies,
Although the wind is east,
Have come in their furs and wrappers,
To watch their charges feast;
To smile and be condescending,
Put pudding on pauper plates,
To be hosts at the workhouse banquet
They've paid for—with the rates.

Oh, the paupers are meek and lowly
With their "Thank'ee kindly, mum's"
So long as they fill their stomachs,
What matter it whence it comes?
But one of the old men mutters,
And pushes his plate aside:
"Great God!" he cries: "but it chokes me!
For this is the day *she* died."

The guardians gazed in horror,
The master's face went white;
"Did a pauper refuse the pudding?"
"Could their ears believe aright?"
Then the ladies clutched their husbands,
Thinking the man would die,
Struck by a bolt, or something,
By the outraged One on high . . .[182]

George Robert Sims (1847–1922), English journalist.
Opening stanzas of a much-parodied dramatic monologue
protesting the life of the poor.

182. *Parlour Poetry*, p. 122.

Hope of All

A little child,
A shining star.
A stable rude,
The door ajar,
Yet in this place,
So crude, forlorn,
The hope of all
The world was born.[183]

Anonymous.

---

183. Chaudhuri, *Carols*, p. 148.

Snail Christmas

Of Orient there were three snails
Who followed ancient Bedouin trails
To see the birth at Bethlehem
Their names were Nathan, Gar, and Shem.
They crept behind the shining star,
The going slow, the distance far
And came just thirteen years too late
(the gospels don't record their fate)
But lucky Nathan, Shem, and Gar
Were present at the Bar Mitzvah.[184]

Anonymous.

184. Percy, *New Articles*, p. 82.

little tree

little tree
little silent Christmas tree
you are so little
you are more like a flower
who found you in the green forest

and were you very sorry to come away?
see i will comfort you because you smell so sweetly
i will kiss your cool bark
and hug you safe and tight
just as your mother would,
only don't be afraid

look the spangles
that sleep all the year in a dark box
dreaming of being taken out and allowed to shine,
the balls the chains red and gold the fluffy threads,

put up your little arms
and i'll give them all to you to hold
every finger shall have its ring
and there won't be a single place dark or unhappy

then when you're quite dressed
you'll stand in the window for everyone to see
and how they'll stare!
oh but you'll be very proud

and my little sister and i will take hands
and looking up at our beautiful tree
we'll dance and sing
"Noel Noel"[185]

e. e. cummings (1894–1962), American poet.

185. Brooks-Davies, *Christmas Please!*, p. 26.

God Rest Ye, Unitarians

God rest ye, Unitarians, let nothing you dismay;
Remember there's no evidence there was a Christmas Day;
When Christ was born is just not known, no matter what they say,
O, Tidings of reason and fact, reason and fact,
Glad tidings of reason and fact.

Our current Christmas customs come from Persia and from
    Greece,
From solstice celebrations of the ancient Middle East.
This whole darn Christmas spiel is just another pagan feast,
O, Tidings of reason and fact, reason and fact,
Glad tidings of reason and fact.

There was no star of Bethlehem, there was no angels' song;
There couldn't have been wise men for the trip would take too long.
The stories in the Bible are historically wrong,
O, Tidings of reason and fact, reason and fact,
Glad tidings of reason and fact.

Christopher G. Raible, Unitarian minister.
Parody of the carol "God rest you merry, gentlemen".

Christmas Card Verse

Carols and candles aglow in the night,
Hearth fires blazing all cosy and bright,
Red-leaved poinsettia, white Christmas rose,
Ice-skaters whirling on ice as it snows,
Sleigh-bells and Santas, Tinsel-trimmed trees,
Mistletoe magic and warm memories,
Angels all bringing glad tidings anew,
Season's best wishes especially for you!

Christmas is a "Clause" for celebration!

May your stocking be brimming with gifts
That come Boxing day you'll not need to thrift.

Christmas season is nigh
And winter is taking hold
So may our wishes keep you dry
And warm you in the cold.

The crinkle of wrapping and the scent of roast
The thoughts of your loved ones and chestnuts to toast
May your Christmas be filled with glee
And thoughts of us and our family.

Like the wings of a dove
May your Christmas be full of love

Hark, the pearly air is trembling,
Liquid music floats along,
Angels in sweet joy assembling,
Thrill the skies with heavenly song.
"Peace on Earth" is their refrain;
O, be it yours this peace to gain.

Santa is loading his sleigh right this minute,
And he's including some gifts for you in it.
But before the big night is finally here,
We wanted to send you some holiday cheer.

THE ART OF CHRISTMAS

Fra Angelico: *The Annunciation* (c. 1440–1445), Convent of San Marco, Florence.

Botticelli: *The Mystical Nativity* (c. 1500–1501), National Gallery, London.

Albrecht Durer: *Adoration of the Magi* (1504), Uffizi Art Gallery, Florence.

Giorgione: *The Adoration of the Shepherds* (1505–1510), National Gallery of Art, Washington DC.

Pieter Bruegel the Elder: *The Census at Bethlehem* (1566), Musées Royaux des Beaux-Arts de Belgique, Brussels.

Orazio Gentileschi: *Rest on the Flight to Egypt* (c. 1620), Birmingham Art Gallery, England.

Nicolas Poussin: *Massacre of the Holy Innocents* (1625–1632), Musée Condé, Chantilly, France.

Philippe de Champaigne: *The Dream of St. Joseph* (1642–1643), National Gallery, London.

Georges de la Tour: *The Newborn Child* (1645–1648), Musée des Beaux-Arts, Rennes, France.

Rembrandt van Rijn: *Simeon in the Temple* (c. 1669), Nationalmuseum, Stockholm, Sweden (the artist's last, unfinished painting).

A CLASSICAL CHRISTMAS

William Byrd: *O magnum mysterium,* 1607.

J. S. Bach: *Magnificat,* 1723.

J. S. Bach: *Christmas Oratorio,* 1734.

Georg Frideric Handel: *Messiah,* 1741.

Hector Berlioz: *L'Enfance du Christ,* 1854.

Tchaikovsky: *Nutcracker Suite,* 1892.

Benjamin Britten: *A Ceremony of Carols,* 1942.

Olivier Messiaen: *Vingt regards sur l'enfant-Jésus,* 1944.

Christmas Prayers

Let the Just Rejoice!

Let the just rejoice, for their Justifier is born.
Let the sick and infirm rejoice, for their Savior is born.
Let the captives rejoice, for their Redeemer is born.
Let slaves rejoice, for their Master is born.
Let free men rejoice, for their Liberator is born.
Let all Christians rejoice, for Jesus Christ is born.

Augustine of Hippo (354–440), church father, author of *The City of God* and *Confessions*.

You have come to us

You have come to us as a small child,
But you have brought us the greatest of all gifts,
The gift of eternal love.
Caress us with Your tiny hands,
Embrace us with Your tiny arms,
And pierce our hearts with Your soft, sweet cries.[186]

Bernard of Clairvaux (1090–1153)

186. Johnson, *Remembering*, p. 68.

Out of Darkness

May God, who has called us out of darkness into his marvelous light, bless us and fill us with peace. Amen.[187]

Church of England

187

A Christmas Prayer

Loving Father,
help us remember the birth of Jesus,
that we may share in the song of the angels,
the gladness of the shepherds,
and worship of the wise men.

Close the door of hate and open the door of love all over the world.
Let kindness come with every gift and good desires with every
   greeting.
Deliver us from evil by the blessing which Christ brings,
and teach us to be merry with clear hearts.

May the Christmas morning make us happy to be thy children,
and the Christmas evening bring us to our beds
with grateful thoughts, forgiving and forgiven,
for Jesus' sake.
Amen.[188]

Attributed to Robert Louis Stevenson (1850–1894), Scots author,
best known for *Treasure Island* and *The Strange Case of Dr Jekyll
and Mr Hyde.*

---

188. Johnson, *Christmas*, p. 54.

Moonless Darkness

Moonless darkness stands between.
Past, the Past, no more be seen!
But the Bethlehem-star may lead me
To the sight of Him Who freed me
From the self that I have been.
Make me pure, Lord: thou art holy;
Make me meek, Lord: thou wert lowly;
Now beginning, and alway:
Now begin, on Christmas day.[189]

Gerard Manley Hopkins (1844–1889), English poet and priest.

189. Phillips, *Hopkins*, p. 77.

A Christmas Prayer for Lonely Folks

Lord God of the solitary.
Look upon me in my loneliness.
Since I may not keep this Christmas in the home,
Send it into my heart.[190]

Henry van Dyke Jr. (1852–1933).

---

190. Van Dyke: *Spirit of Christmas*, p. 56.

Little Child of Love

Good Jesus,
born at this time,
a little child of love for us;
be born in me
so that I may be
a little child in love with you.[191]

Edward Bouverie Pusey (1800–1882), English cleric.

191. *Essential Christmas Prayers*, p. 22.

Bidding Prayer

Beloved in Christ, at this Christmas-tide, let it be our care and delight to hear again the message of the angels, and in heart and mind to go even unto Bethlehem and see this thing which is come to pass, and the Babe lying in a manger.

Therefore let us read and mark in Holy Scripture the tale of the loving purposes of God from the first days of our disobedience unto the glorious Redemption brought us by this Holy Child.

But first, let us pray for the needs of the whole world; for peace on earth and goodwill among all his people; for unity and brotherhood within the Church he came to build . . .

And because this would rejoice his heart, let us remember, in his name, the poor and helpless, the cold, the hungry, and the oppressed; the sick and them that mourn, the lonely and the unloved, the aged and the little children; and all those who know not the Lord Jesus, or who love him not, or who by sin have grieved his heart of love.

Lastly, let us remember before God all those who rejoice with us, but upon another shore, and in a greater light, that multitude which no one can number, whose hope was in the Word made flesh, and with whom in the Lord Jesus we are one for evermore.[192]

Eric Milner-White (1884–1963), who devised the Festival of Nine Lessons and Carols held annually on Christmas Eve at King's College, Cambridge, England.

192. Jacques, *Carols*, p. 176.

FIRST CHRISTMAS POSTAGE STAMPS

1898: Canadian stamp with the inscription "XMAS 1898".

1935: British troops in Egypt issued stamp overprinted "Xmas 1935".

1937: Austria issued two Christmas stamps, with rose and zodiac signs.

1939: Brazil issued four stamps, featuring the three kings, an angel and child, the Southern Cross and a child, and a mother and child.

1943: Hungary issued stamps depicting the Nativity.

1951: Cuba issued designs with poinsettias and bells.

1962: First U.S. Christmas stamps.

1966: First U.K. Christmas stamps.

Bibliography

Alcott, Louisa May. *Little Women*, Harmondsworth: Penguin, 1994.

Anon. *Essential Christmas Prayers*. Brewster, Mass.: Paraclete, 2017.

Anon. *This England's Book of Parlour Poetry*. This England: Cheltenham, 1989.

Armstrong, John Regis and J. A. Wayne Hellmann, eds. *Francis of Assisi. Early Documents*, Vol. II. New York: New City, 2002.

Barkworth, Peter, ed. *For All Occasions: Poems, Prose and Party Pieces for Reading Aloud*. London: Methuen, 1999.

Batchelor, Mary, ed. *A Treasury of Christian Poetry*. New York: Gramercy Books, 2004.

Beaglehole, John Cawte, ed. *The Endeavour Journal of Joseph Banks 1768–1771*. Sydney: Angus & Robertson, 1962.

Beeching, Henry Charles, ed. *A Book of Christmas Verse*. London: Humphrey Milford, 1926.

Beerbohm, Max. *A Christmas Garland*. London: William Heinemann, 1922.

Beeton, Isabella Mary. *Mrs Beeton's Book of Household Management*. Abridged edition. Oxford: Oxford University Press, 2000.

Bella, Leslie. *The Christmas Imperative: Leisure, Family, and Women's Work*. Halifax: Fernwood, 1992.

Blind, Mathilde. *Songs and Sonnets*. London: Chatto & Windus, 1893.

Brandreth, Gyles. *On Christmas*. London: Notting Hill, 2017.

Brooks-Davies, Douglas. *Christmas Please! One Hundred Poems for the Festive Season*. London: Phoenix, 2000.

Brooks, Phillips. *Christmas Songs and Easter Carols*. New York: E. P. Dutton, 1903.

Brown, Cameron. *Christmas Facts, Figures & Fun*. London: Facts, Figures & Fun, 2005.

Bullen, A. H., ed. *A Christmas Garland*. London: John C. Nimmo, 1885.

Cain, Tom and Ruth Connolly, eds. *The Poems of Ben Jonson*. London: Routledge, 2022.

Carroll, Lewis. *The Complete Works of Lewis Carroll*. London: Nonesuch, 1939.

Chadhuri, Prabir Rai. *Christmas Carols & Christmas Wishes*. Prabir Rai Chadhuri, 2022.

Chesterton, Frances. *How Far to Bethlehem and Other Carols*. London: Sheed & Ward, 1927.

Chesterton, G. K. *The Spirit of Christmas*. Marie Smith ed. London: Xanadu, 1984.

Chitham, Edward. *The Poems of Anne Brontë: A New Text and Commentary*. London: Macmillan, 1979.

Clayton, Thomas, ed. *The Works of Sir John Suckling*. Oxford: Clarendon Press, 1971.

Coffin, William Sloane and Helen A. & Clarence Dickinson eds. *The Coming of the Prince of Peace: A Nativity Play with Ancient Christmas Carols*. New York: H. W. Gray, 1920.

Coleridge, Ernest Hartley ed. *The Poetical Works of Samuel Taylor Coleridge*. London: Henry Frowde, 1912.

Crump, R. W. ed. *The Complete Poems of Christina Rossetti Vol. II*. Baton Rouge: Louisiana State University Press, 1986.

Cummings, E. E. *Tulips & Chimneys*. New York: Thomas Seltzer, 1923.

Davies, R. T., ed. *Medieval English Lyrics: A Critical Anthology*. London: Faber and Faber, 1963.

de Beer, Edmund Samuel, ed. *The Diary of John Evelyn*. London: Oxford University Press, 1959.

Dearmer, Percy, R., et al. eds. *The Oxford Book of Carols*. London: Oxford University Press, 1928.

Dickens, Charles. *A Christmas Carol*. London: Vintage, 2017.

———. *Great Expectations*. Oxford: Oxford University Press, 1953.

———. *Selected Short Fiction*. London: Penguin, 1976.

———. *Sketches by Boz. Vol I*. London: Chapman & Hall, 1898.

———. *The Pickwick Papers*. London: Penguin, 2003.

Dunbar, Paul Laurence. *Poems of Cabin and Field*. New York: Dodd, Mead, 1899.

Eliot, George. *The Mill on the Floss*. London: Penguin, 1985.

Gardner, Helen, ed. *The New Oxford Book of English Verse 1250–1950*. London: Book Club Associates, 1975.

Gibbons, Stella. *Christmas at Cold Comfort Farm*. London: Vintage, 2011.

Gosse, Edmund. *Father and Son: A Study of Two Temperaments*. Harmondsworth: Penguin, 1983.

Grahame, Kenneth. *The Wind in the Willows*. London: Kestrel, 1983.

Grosart, Alexander Balloch, ed. *The Complete Works of Richard Crashaw*. Vol. I. London: Robson, 1872.

Grossmith, George and Weedon. *The Diary of a Nobody*. Ware, Hertfordshire: Wordsworth, 1994.

Hadfield, Miles and John. *The Twelve Days of Christmas*. London: Cassell, 1961.

Hardy, Thomas. *Under the Greenwood Tree: or The Mellstock Quire*. London: Macmillan, 1920

Hayward, John ed. *John Donne: A Selection of his Poetry*. Harmondsworth, Penguin, 1950.

Heinz, Donald. *Christmas: Festival of Incarnation*. Minneapolis: Fortress, 2010.

Holland, Josiah Gilbert. *The Complete Poetical Writings*. New York: Charles Scribner's Sons, 1879.

Howse, Christopher, ed. *Best Sermons Ever*. London: Continuum, 2001.

Hyett, Florence B., ed. *Fifty Christmas Poems for Children*. Oxford: Basil Blackwell, 1923.

Hymns Ancient & Modern: New Standard Full Music Edition. Norwich: Hymns Ancient and Modern, 1983.

Hymns of Faith. London: Scripture Union, 1964.

Hynes, Samuel, ed. *The Complete Poetical Works of Thomas Hardy* Vol II. Oxford: Oxford University Press, 1964.

Jacques, Reginald and David Willcocks, eds. *Carols for Choirs: Fifty Christmas Carols*. London: Oxford University Press, 1961.

James, Henry. *English Hours*. London: Tauris Parke, 2011.

Jenkins, Harold, ed. *The Arden Shakespeare: Hamlet*. London: Methuen, 1982.

Johnson Dennis L., ed. *Remembering That It Happened Once: Christmas Carmen for Spiritual Life*. Seattle: Wipf & Stock, 2021.

Johnson, Greg. *The 25 Days of Christmas*. Nashville, Tenn: Thomas Nelson, 2004.

Keyte, Hugh and Andrew Parrott, eds. *The Shorter New Oxford Book of Carols*. Oxford: Oxford University Press, 1993.

Latham, Robert, ed. *The Diary of Samuel Pepys: A Selection*. London: Penguin, 1987.

Lawrence, D. H.; Helen Baron and Carl Baron, eds. *Sons and Lovers*. Cambridge: Cambridge University Press, 1992.

Lawrence, D. H.; Mark Kinkead-Weekes ed. *The Rainbow*. Cambridge: Cambridge University Press, 1989.

Lawson-Jones, Mark. *Why was the Partridge in the Pear Tree: The History of Christmas Carols*. Cheltenham: History Press, 2011.

Leather, Eleanor Mary, "Scraps of English Folklore, XIV, Herefordshire", in *Folklore* 37:3 (September 30 1926) 297.

Lee, Laurie. *Cider with Rosie*. London: Hogarth, 1959.

Levi, Peter, ed. *The Penguin Book of English Christian Verse*. Penguin: Harmondsworth, 1984.

Lewis, D. B. Wyndham and G. C. Heseltine eds. *A Christmas Book: An Anthology for Moderns*. London: J. M. Dent, 1931.

Macdonald, Lyn. *1914–18: Voices and Images of the Great War*. Harmondsworth: Michael Joseph, 1988.

Marsh, Jan, ed. *Christina Rossetti*. London: J. M. Dent, 1996.

Martin, L. C., ed. *The Poetical Works of Robert Herrick*. Oxford: Clarendon Press, 1956.

Mather, Increase. *Testimony Against Prophane Customs*. Charlottesville: University of Virginia, 1953.

McGonagall, William. *Collected Poems*. Edinburgh: Birlinn, 1992.

Misson, Henri de Valbourg. *Misson's Memoirs and Observations in His Travels Over England*, transl. John Ozell. London: Browne, 1719.

Moore, Clement C. *The Night Before Christmas*. London: George C. Harrap, 1932.

Moran, Donald N. "Early American Christmases." *The Barnes Review*, Washington DC, (November/December 2010), 4–5.

Northern Advertiser, The. Western Australia (5 March 1938).

Percy, Martyn. *Thirty-Nine New Articles: An Anglican Landscape of Faith*. Norwich: Canterbury, 2013.

Phillips, Catherine, ed. *Gerard Manley Hopkins: The Major Works*. Oxford: Oxford University Press, 2002.

Plomer William, ed. *Kilvert's Diary 1870–1879*. London: Vintage, 2013.

Potter, Beatrix. *The Tailor of Gloucester*. London: Frederick Warne, 1903.

Quiller-Couch, Arthur, ed. *The Oxford Book Of English Verse 1250–1900*: Oxford: Oxford University Press, 1900.

Ramsey, Boniface, transl. *The Sermons of St. Maximus of Turin*. New York: Newman, 1989.

Roosevelt, Franklin D. Library: First Carbon Files 1933–1945: National Archives Identifier: 197366.

Sandys, William. *Christmastide: its History, Festivities, and Carols*. London: John Russell Smith, 1852.

Santich, Barbara, ed. *In the Land of the Magic Pudding: A Gastronomic Miscellany*. Adelaide: Wakefield, 2000.

Scott, Rivers, ed. *No Man is an Island: A Selection From the Prose of John Donne*. London: Folio Society, 1997.

Scott, Robert F. *The Voyage of the "Discovery"*. London: Smith, Elder, 1907.

Shakespeare, William; Harold Jenkins, ed. *Hamlet*. London: Routledge 1982.

Shaw, George Bernard. *Music in London 1890–1894*. Vol. III. London: Constable, 1932.

Shoemaker, Alfred Lewis. *Christmas in Pennsylvania: A Folk-Cultural Study*. Mechanicsburg, Pennsylvania: Stackpole, 1999.

Slater, Michael, ed. *Dickens' Journalism* VI: *Sketches by Boz*. London: J. M. Dent, 1994.

Smith, Godfrey. *The Christmas Reader*. London: Viking, 1985.

Tennyson, Alfred Lord. Christopher Ricks ed. *The Poems of Tennyson*. London: Longmans, 1969.

The American Scholar. Washington DC: Phi Beta Kappa (7 December 2015).

The Book of Common Prayer. Cambridge: John Baskerville, 1662.

Trollope, Anthony. *Orley Farm*. London: The Trollope Society, 1990.

Van Dyke, Henry. *The Spirit of Christmas*. New York: Charles Scribner, 1905.

William Tyndale's New Testament. Wordsworth Editions, Ware, 2002.

Williams, George Walton, ed. *The Complete Poetry of Richard Crashaw*. New York: New York University, 1972.

Winstanley, R. L., ed. *The Ansford Diary of James Woodforde*. N.P.: Parson Woodford Society, 1988.

Index of Titles

Index of Authors

Index of First Lines

Milton Keynes UK
Ingram Content Group UK Ltd.
UKHW022104060824
446627UK00009B/284

9 798385 212354